Around
Memories of Sparkh

Frances Wilmot

First published
by Brewin Books, Studley, Warwickshire, B80 7LG
in September 1993

Reprinted February 1994

ISBN 1 85858 025 0

British Library Cataloguing in Publication Data.
A Catalogue record for this book is available from the British Library

Typeset in Plantin by Avon Dataset, Bidford on Avon, Warwickshire, B50 4JH
and made and printed by Supaprint (Redditch) Limited.

Acknowledgements

Grateful acknowledgements are due to the following persons, organisations and periodicals:-

D. M. Abbott; Acocks Green Local History Society; K. Aitken; J. Alder; B. Ashworth; F. Baldry; M. Barnes; Barrows Stores Ltd; D. Biddle; V. Bird; Birmingham Transport Historical Group; Birmingham Library Services, especially Local Studies Department, Acocks Green and Hall Green Libraries; Birmingham Museums and Art Gallery; L. Blennerhassett (photography); J. Boden; Cadbury Ltd; W. Canning & Co. Ltd; H. Cheshire; M. Clarke; W. N. Dixon; E. Edmonds; E. Farrow; Good Housekeeping; C. Hawkes; Land Worker; J. Marks; Midland Counties Dairymaid; Midland Red; Millbrook House Ltd; Ministry of Food; National Motor Museum; The National Trust; W. H. Painter Ltd; Punch; H. Scott; T. Southwell; St Christopher's (Springfield) Monthly Magazine; St John's (Sparkhill) Parish Magazine; St Mary's (Acocks Green) Parish Magazine; J. R. Taylor; Times Furnishing Ltd; Vogue; Warwick Cinema (Birmingham) Ltd; M.White; John Whybrow Ltd; N. E. S. Wilmot; M. Wood; and my husband Paul who gave much help and support to the project.

Dedicated to my parents, Margaret and Maurice Headford, who lived in Acocks Green for forty six years.

Cover design by K. Aitken

CONTENTS

Chapter 1	Season of Nettles	1
Chapter 2	Twenties Childhood in Sparkhill	5
Chapter 3	Hitchinson's National Plate Works	19
Chapter 4	Chalet Flora	25
Chapter 5	Rising Dreams	31
Chapter 6	The Rise of "4 o'Clock"	37
Chapter 7	Wartime at "4 o'Clock"	47
Chapter 8	Life during the Blitz at "4 o'Clock"	57
Chapter 9	Spring Farm	65
Chapter 10	Around Fox Hollies in Acocks Green	69
Chapter 11	Along the Yardley Road in Acocks Green	77
Chapter 12	Acocks Green in the Days of Horses	89
Chapter 13	Acocks Green from Village to Suburb	99
Chapter 14	Acocks Green Village Centre	117
Chapter 15	Glimpses of Old Sparkhill	133
Chapter 16	Roundabout Camp Hill	147
Chapter 17	Changing Scenes of Life	151

CHAPTER 1

SEASON OF NETTLES

"The season of nettles heralded the birth of Margaret Matilda Hitchinson on the 29th May in 1913", recalled a Yorkshire kinsman. But few nettles grew in Nansen Road in Sparkhill where she was born as it was an expanding suburb on the outskirts of Birmingham. The road of terraced houses was typical of many in the district, being built in late Victorian times. Most houses were without the convenience of bathrooms, toilets or garages. Gardens were long and narrow, mostly cultivating cabbages and other vegetables.

Named after her two grandmothers Margaret Matilda was known as Margo in the family. Her father, Ernest Hitchinson, was an electro-plate manufacturer in Birmingham. Her mother, Miriam Hitchinson, was from the Southwell farming family who had lived for generations in the Yorkshire Wolds. Going back a generation into the nineteenth century, to Ernest and Miriam Hitchinson's parents, both families were worthy members of the Victorian middle class but with very different backgrounds.

Arthur Hitchinson, Margo's paternal grandfather, was well established in Birmingham as a certificated teacher, having worked in several schools in the Birmingham School Board. He had been Chief Assistant at Camden Street Mixed School for over twenty years until his retirement in 1909. Many children probably went to school under-nourished, ragged and barefoot. Free breakfasts were provided in school for the poorest children which consisted of a mug of cocoa, bread and margarine — and jam if they were lucky.

Arthur Hitchinson and his wife Matilda brought up a family of seven children in Sparkhill. Ernest was their fourth child, and eventually formed a partnership with his brother Harry in 1915 — Hitchinson & Co., an electro-plating business specialising in making products for the hotel industry.

Ernest Hitchinson met his wife Miriam Southwell in a manner that was certainly not approved of in those strict Edwardian times — on the Spa Promenade at Scarborough in 1909. Miriam was the eldest daughter of Thomas Southwell, a gentleman farmer at Manor Farm in Thwing, a tiny village on the Yorkshire Wolds. Thomas was a dedicated farmer who eventually retired to Scarborough in 1921, becoming a respected member of the Rural District Council. His wife, Margaret, was from a local farming family. They refused to receive Ernest Hitchinson when he first called to visit their daughter. But eventually an engagement was permitted, and Miriam

1913. Margo Hitchinson as a baby sitting on the lap of her grand-mother, Margaret Southwell, beside her mother, Miriam Hitchinson.

married Ernest on the 31st January 1912 in the little village church of Thwing. A grand wedding tea was given for all parishioners.

Miriam had been born in Thwing and had trained as a children's nurse. Known as 'Tiny' to her husband, she was an large attractive woman and had a happy personality. She was very much in love with her husband which must have helped her to adjust to living in a completely different environment. Sparkhill was on the outer edge of Birmingham but was quite unlike the peaceful rural Yorkshire countryside in which she had grown up. She was far from her family and must have missed her sister Madge, her two brothers Dick and Ben, her parents, her work with children and the close farming community surrounding Thwing.

Ernest's family — his widowed father Arthur, his sister May, brothers Harry, Albert and Tudor — all lived locally in Birmingham. At the time of

A typical farming scene in the Yorkshire Wolds, c.1912. (T. Southwell)

Ernest Hitchinson's marriage to Miriam in 1912 Birmingham was still dominated by horse transport until the beginning of the First World War. When Lord Kitchener commandeered many of the best horses for service in France, city streets changed dramatically with the disappearance of the open-topped horse-buses which travelled down the Stratford Road towards Sparkhill. Competition with the railways and the introduction of motor transport and trams soon caused a rapid decline in horse-drawn vehicles of all types. It was a period of great social change with new mechanical novelties, domestic gadgets of all kinds and electricity in homes. The middle classes began to commute to work on electric trams into the town centre while living on the outer suburbs in areas such as Sparkhill.

Margo was born in the year following her parent's marriage in 1913 and was an only child. They made regular visits to the Southwells in Yorkshire so Margo developed a very close relationship with her grandmother, Margaret Southwell, and her Aunt Madge. Her Uncle Dick, who farmed Spring Farm in Thorpe Bassett, always remembered her birthday when the nettles came out as he had been told the news of 'our Mirrie's baby' when he was out cutting down the weeds on the farm.

Throughout her life Margo Headford (nee Hitchinson) always enjoyed writing. This book has been made possible by using some of her material which was passed on to her daughters when she went into a nursing home in

The horse bus on the Stratford Road, near Farm Road, heading for the Mermaid Hotel in Sparkhill, c.1912. (Birmingham Library Services)

1989. Many contemporary friends have also contributed their reminiscences of the area and much additional historical research has been made to set the scene of her very interesting and active life in the provinces of south Birmingham and further afield, especially in the Twenties, Thirties and Forties. Additional research reveals the local history and development of Sparkhill and Acocks Green, which goes back past the nineteenth century.

CHAPTER 2

TWENTIES CHILDHOOD IN SPARKHILL

Parcels of butter arriving by post were one of Margo Hitchinson's earliest memories of life at Number 76 Nansen Road in Sparkhill. Her grandparents, Thomas and Margaret Southwell, sent the butter from their farm in Yorkshire during the First World War. Butter was a rationed commodity, along with cheese, margarine and meat, having doubled in price during the war years when blockades of ships caused food shortages. No doubt Margo's mother, Miriam, was delighted to have an addition to the family's rations with all the problems of feeding and clothing a family in wartime.

Government slogans like 'Eat slowly' and 'Keep warm' were common in 1918 when housewives were spending hours each day in all weathers, queueing and struggling to different shops for essential foods. Everyone was encouraged to eat lots of porridge, pulses and steamed suet puddings.

Housekeeping was a trial as prices rose daily. For example, between 1914 – 18 prices for meat, soap, matches, eggs and tea had more than doubled in price. Although Miriam Hitchinson did not contribute to the war effort in any other way she was one of millions who fought the war at home by looking after the family. Children were also expected to do their bit by collecting silver paper, rags and wool for the war effort.

The Ministry of Munitions war slogan of 1918 was "work, work, turn out shells!" so that every effort was made in Birmingham to match the Artillery's demands. Ernest Hitchinson, Margo's father, made munitions along with his own electro-plate ware in his factory in Legge Lane. Women were to be seen everywhere, from munition making to driving the new motor buses which were more flexible than electric trams and quicker than horse buses. The requisitioning of horses for the war left motor buses triumphant.

As an antidote to war the cinema became well established as the 'poor man's theatre' although film programmes were very short. There was a tremendous advance in technology from the early flickering films which resulted in the improvement of picture theatre buildings and the development of the musical side of the programmes. They became known grandly as 'picture palaces' with luxurious seats, the music almost being a rival to the films, with orchestras and organs in the bigger Birmingham cinemas. Sparkhill was fortunate to have the Savoy and the Springfield which entertained many people in the Twenties.

By 1918, when Margo was five years old, there was great joy at the end of

1916. Margo Hitchinson in black stockings, aged 3, with her mother, Miriam.

FINISHING SHELL-CASES

TAPER BATH WITH HIGH BACK.   OXFORD HIP BATHS

Typical baths of the period.

76, *Nansen Road, Sparkhill.*

the war, followed by years of unemployment in Birmingham. But Nansen Road was Margo's world, as she wrote:-

I was fortunate to live in one of the six houses in Nansen Road to have a bathroom. On the wall of our terraced house was a plaque which said 'Grove Park Villas', which indicated it had been built on the estate of Grove Farm about 1900. Most of the houses were painted in sombre brown colours.

My best friend, Joan Baldry, lived at Number 124 at the top of the road where there was no bathroom. Somewhere in the scullery a bath was secreted away and the family of five had to take it in turns to have a bath from time to time. Another friend had a carpenter for a father who made an ingenious contraption which lifted the bath up and down out of its cupboard. We were lucky in that we just stepped out of the scullery for the toilet but most people had to go further outside before they could ease themselves which must have been cold in winter. The toilet was known as the 'W.C.'.

There were no self-service shops in the Twenties — everyone had to queue up at the counter to ask for their goods. Biscuits, sugar and flour were weighed. Butter was sliced and patted into shape before being wrapped. Goods could be delivered to your door, if requested, which was a great boon to housewives. Many tradesmen, such as the baker and greengrocer, came regularly to our home with their horse and cart. Milk was usually sold from horse-drawn milk carts in big metal churns, the

Nansen Rd, Sparkhill — a peaceful 'horse-road', built about 1900. The road is typical of many in the area. (J. Marks)

amount being measured into a metal container before being poured into the customer's jug.

Sparkhill Picture Palace, later called the Savoy, was at the bottom of Nansen Road on the Stratford Road. It had opened in 1911 and admission was 3d or 6d, with seats for over five hundred people. My mother spent many an hour watching Pearl White, Rudolf Valentino, Douglas Fairbanks, Greta Garbo and other film stars of the day. My Aunt Madge idolized Valentino, as did millions of other women. Another local cinema was the Springfield which was thought to be considerably 'up-market'.

I began my education at College Road School which still looks much the same from the outside. The school was the last built by Yardley School Board in 1900 and the first to have a central hall. I attended this school with my friend, Joan Baldry, who became one of the three life-long friends I made in Nansen Road.

Our local playground was Nansen Road, the "horse-road" as it was called, which had very little traffic. Our local milkman, Mr Batchelor, lived up the road and delivered the milk in a large can. If we ran short we only had to go up the road to fetch some more. I remember once being sent there with a large milk jug. On the way back I broke the jug and arrived back home still carrying the handle!

None of the families living in Nansen road had a car until my father bought a Bean, a very heavy motor car which was made to last. It was

The 11.9 BEAN TWO-SEATER

With Dickey Seat and
All-Weather Side Curtains.

£335

Bean family car.

Bodywork constructed of thoroughly seasoned hardwood, panelled in silver steel finished off in
aluminium moulding. A particularly comfortable and wide front seat and substantially constructed Dickey are provided. Upholstered in a variety (to choice) of genuine first quality leathers.
Painted to choice of four colours, or finished in the new aluminium "curl polish." Fitted with
All-weather Side Curtains.

Bean ad.

manufactured by A. Harper Sons and Bean who sold cars in the
Twenties, rather suffering from the competition with the popular Morris
and Austin Twelve models on the market. The car was garaged on the
Stratford Road as there were no garages in Nansen road. The Bean was
only used for pleasure and was always a source of wonder to our
neighbours. But I remember my aunt being horrified to find my father
trying to repair a tyre on the kitchen table as there were few garages
around in those days.

We were envied by everyone as we set off in the Bean, named 'Tiny',
for jaunts in the countryside with my friend Joan and myself sitting in
the open 'dickey' at the back. My mother loved the outings into the
Warwickshire countryside which was not far away in those days when
motoring was a pleasure on deserted roads. She used to wear a long
leather coat and loved the tiny country villages which reminded her of her
home on the Yorkshire Wolds.

Cars became a status symbol in the inter-war years while motor coaches
or charabancs rivalled the express trains for excursions to the seaside. The
death toll on the roads rose alarmingly as there were no driving schools
or tests for drivers.

The countryside was very near to Sparkhill in those days. We only had
to walk up Shaftmoor Lane and get to Spring Road where we were
among green fields. Fox Hollies Road was a country lane in my
childhood, with many elm trees.

Children and elderly people were quite safe to go around on their own.
Young people used to congregate to meet on 'The Hill' on the Stratford
Road near Sparkhill Park, the area known as the 'Monkey Run', and
there was a thriving youth club at St Christopher's church.

I qualified in 1924 for a scholarship at King Edward VI's Grammar
School in Camp Hill where I went with Ethel Baldwin, a friend who lived
nearby in Oakwood Road. Our school uniform consisted of mini-length

K.E.G.S., Camphill.

gym slips worn with a blouse and tie and the dreaded itchy black woollen stockings. School was very strict where we had to learn lots of tables and English grammar and had much homework. We had few games lessons although there were new horizontal bars in the gym in 1926. Netball and tennis was taught, the latter developing into a life-long passion for me. We were divided into four 'houses' — Pioneers, Eagles, Swifts and Ironsides. Each house organised socials when there were competitions such as egg and spoon races, obstacle races and tennis tournaments.

The boys and girls had quite separate establishments. Once a party of girls cycled to the Lickeys for a view of the eclipse in 1926. Other excursions to Wales and Paris were options which I was unable to take up as by then my father's business was struggling and there was no spare money for such luxuries.

I usually travelled to school by tram which cost me one penny but I often walked to save the money. In the General Strike of 1926 I once got a lift in a Rolls Royce as there were no trams running on the Stratford Road. In 1927 a new wing opened where there was a new chemistry laboratory, a domestic science room and a lecture hall. Many years later in the Sixties the building became Bordesley College of Education.

Margo's school friend Ethel Baldwin, with whom she founded her Acocks Green business venture in 1936, has memories of her early life in Oakwood Road in Sparkhill:-

My father, Arthur Baldwin, was a schoolmaster and became Head of Stechford Council School. We were a family of seven and lived in Oakwood Road where our garden backed on to Sparkhill Park. There was a brook running all along the bottom of our garden and the neighbouring gardens which was our paradise. There was often the added excitement of an occasional cry of "He's fallen in!!" and all the mothers from nearby would go rushing down their gardens to rescue their children from a watery death!

The highlight of the week was when my mother went shopping late on Saturday night on the Stratford Road. All perishable foods had to be sold quickly then as there were no fridges in those days. The butcher sold his meat cheaply and cakes and bread were reduced at Holtom's bakery. As I was one of five children treats were few so Saturday nights were special, when we had fruit and cakes to eat.

Sometimes in the spring my mother used to buy bunches of mimosa

K.E.G.S., Camp Hill, 1925. Front row: Margo Hitchinson (in plaits) and Ethel Baldwin (2nd from left).

which I thought was magical as the lovely colours and the soft damp scented blossom thrilled me.

Our pocket money was tuppence a week which we often spent at a small general store at the bottom of our road. There we had to make the great decision of how to spend it — a halfpenny a time or splash out and spend it all?!! Another treat was paying the milk bill at the same shop when Mrs Shepherd usually gave us a small bag of broken biscuits. If she was too busy or had no biscuits we came out feeling really cheated. I have often wondered since whether we qualified as 'deprived children' — there is no doubt we should have been in that category by today's standards!

An annual event that I remember in the Twenties was the illuminated tram which came along the Stratford Road as far as College Road. It was a vision of warmth and bright lights and was often preceded and followed by an army of tramway men in fancy dress costumes, collecting for the Lord Mayor's Distress Fund.

There were shops and businesses of all kinds on the Stratford Road near Nansen Road, including George Mason the grocer, several drapers, bakers and butchers, George Baker the milliner, the Birmingham Industrial Co-op grocers, Thomas Selvey the artificial teeth-maker, Ernest Slade the bazaar, two dairies and John Snell the hosier.

In the Twenties many shops were similar to this sketch. (Punch, 1903)

Frank Baldry, brother of Margo's friend Joan, remembers John Snell's shop which supplied his father-in-law with many pairs of spats. The firm specialised in mens' and boyswear, selling many caps in the Twenties, remaining in Sparkhill for many years. Frank Baldry, who lived in Nansen Road, recalls many of the residents in his boyhood in the Twenties:-

I can remember especially Mr Fowler who lived at the top of the road. He was quite a character and built a garage in his garden in which to keep his motorbike and sidecar. It was quite a sight to see him moving mature trees on his sidecar. He waterproofed his garage with hot molten tar, resulting in disaster one day when the tar cooking on his kitchen stove caught fire!

Sparkhill Park was the centre of our sporting activities after graduating from street games. However, the park-keeper did not permit the use of a football so we had to go to Formans Road Recreation ground for a game of football. The River Cole near the Stratford Road provided an adventurous area as did the Dingles between the Stratford Road and Trittiford Park. Cycling was also a popular activity with clubs. Those of us who cycled in those days think ourselves lucky to have enjoyed quiet country roads, before motorists made it unpleasant.

Stratford Road in my childhood was a very busy shopping centre with shops spreading from Formans Road to Springfield, the last one being an ironmongers on the outer edge of Birmingham. As a contrast, other roads such as Woodlands Road were bordered by hilly fields on one side.

The noisy trams made a big impression on us as a family as we had just moved from quieter Lincoln in 1921. My mother never thought she would get used to the din! The Number 21 tram had its terminus at College Road.

The 1931 hurricane also remains in my memory, blowing along the Cole Valley and especially in Formans Road. Many roofs were blown off, and baths and dustbins were scattered around the district.

Good Housekeeping advertisements, 1924 – 1926.

J. J. Snell's shop for men's and boy's wear, at No. 738 Stratford Road, Sparkhill (near Formans Road) in the Twenties. (J. Marks)

Glancing through the *Birmingham Advertiser* for 1922/3 gives us many glimpses of contemporary life, with articles being written about allotment culture, poultry keeping and many labour-saving devices for busy housewives. Advice was given to keep meat, fish and milk on a cold slate or marble shelf. One article stated that "old-fashioned kitchens often resembled dungeons, rather than hygienic places to cook" and suggested using the new gas or electricity supply. It was realised for the first time that bathrooms and kitchens were an important part of the house. An increase in the number of gas explosions in the district led to an inquiry into the quality of gas being supplied to households for domestic use.

The popularity of Midland Red Motor Bus services was reported to "be almost phenomenal to meet the needs of the public". The service covered most of the districts in the Midlands with many pleasant runs into the country for special events such as 'blossom-time'. Many newspaper articles on seaside resorts encouraged the trend for travel.

The 'tuppenny tram ride' was described in the newspaper as being "fascinating to a student of humanity, when riding upstairs at night while all the shops were lit up. Watch the tram men with their steaming mugs of tea and cocoa and great sandwiches and hunks of cake. They have a way of hoisting old ladies aboard, shepherding school boys aloft, explaining the fare to deaf people and singing out 'pass right down along the car please' which is altogether inimitable and priceless."

Stratford Road trams, with Camp Hill in the distance, in the 1920's. (Birmingham Transport Historical Group)

Midland Red, 1927.

Sparkhill Library.

A big event in Sparkhill took place on January 19th 1923 when the Public Library opened in Yardley District Council House building. The Librarian, Mr G. Burton, was besieged with application forms on opening day, having only a stock of 4,500 books. The children's library was absolutely cleared of books in two weeks and the main library reduced to 1000 books on the shelves. The books were arranged on the new open-access system where borrowers could choose for themselves.

In 1926, when Margo Hitchinson was thirteen years old, her mother Miriam became seriously ill with stomach cancer and was nursed at home. She was unable to eat very much at the end, despite her love of food, and left a poignant letter to her daughter before she died: "Mother wants you to grow up to be a real good woman and a comfort to all around . . . comfort and look after Daddy, Gran and Granpa and try to take my place in their hearts as they love you very dearly. Try to think of me as out of pain and happy. . . God bless you always. . ."

She died in February 1927 at the age of forty one, her ashes being buried in Beoley churchyard, a little village visited and admired on motoring trips where her husband knew the vicar. The church is still in the countryside and is a peaceful spot, surrounded by the sound of rooks in the tall trees. A small plaque marked the grave: "Mirrie Hitchinson of Thwing, E. Yorks, lived 15 happy years in Birmingham as wife, then mother. Loved by all who knew her."

A sister of Margo's Aunt Nellie came to keep house for Margo Hitchinson and her father for three years after Miriam's death. During this time Margo worked hard at school and passed her Matriculation. She left school to get a job in those days of ever lengthening dole queues as a clerk in a city opticians, earning the sum of fifteen shillings a week. University was not an option as her father was unable to support her due to his failing business.

Later on Margo left home when her father had remarried, after she had discovered her new stepmother reading her carefully hidden diary into which she had poured out all her unhappy thoughts. She went to live with her Aunt Nellie and Uncle Harry Hitchinson but accepted her father's offer of a job in his electro-plate business in 1931 when she was eighteen years old. She had no real plans for the future, except that she knew she would come into her mother's legacy in three years time.

CHAPTER 3

HITCHINSON'S NATIONAL PLATE WORKS

Legge Lane is in Birmingham's Jewellery Quarter where the very rich and the desperately poor often rubbed shoulders in 1931, when jobs were scarce and wages low. Footpads were reputed to haunt the area and there were many scrawny cats around, no doubt pursuing the rats from the local brook. It was not a particularly good place for a young woman to go on her own but Margo Hitchinson was glad of the offer of work at £1 per week in her father's business.

The business, 'Hitchinson & Co., National Plate Works', had been founded at Number 3 in 1915, by Ernest Hitchinson and his brother Harry. They manufactured electro-plate ware for the hotel industry. It was a fine three storey Victorian building, built in 1893 by the architects Essex, Nicol and Goodman, leading exponents of the decorative use of terra-cotta in Birmingham. Designed for Alfred Woodward's Pen and Pen-holder Works, a gable was proudly inscribed "IXL Works. A. H. Woodward, Manufacturer of Patent Pencil Cases etc." It was one of the architects most effective designs, being of red bricks and terra-cotta dressings, decorated with friezes around the windows on the second floor. The building can still be seen today.

Margo recalls her work there for two years:-

My job was to look after the direct sales travellers, checking invoices for silveroid goods sold and the amount of money being received by the firm. A lot of my time was spent answering "the trap" where many callers came for the money for raw materials purchased by the firm. The girl who answered the trap had to be clean and polite as the firm was judged by its employees. No-one knew I was the boss's daughter as he never acknowledged our relationship in "the place", as he always called it.

My father was known as 'Mr Ernest' and was the driving force of the firm. As there was no internal telephone I often had to chase about all over the building to find him as he sorted out all the problems in the factory. My uncle, known as 'Mr Harry', was the travelling representative who visited hotels to find sales for their products, which included tea and coffee services. Knives were proudly inscribed with "The best of its kind, Ernest Hitchinson, Birmingham, Eng."

There was a long noisy wooden flight of stairs leading to the trap and

Ernest Hitchinson's electro-plate business operated in these fine premises which had originally been built in 1893. (Architect, 1893)

my father's office which had bare wooden floors, some show cases, a Gestetner machine and one telephone high up on the wall. The typist used an old manual typewriter and was very efficient.

In the warehouse were long work tables by the window where workers prepared and packed the goods. Some items were beautifully wrapped in waterproof paper for hotels abroad. The parcels were taken up to the stockroom in a simple lift.

Huge baskets on wheels were dotted around for the articles being treated. Burnishing was done by women, mostly middle- aged, dressed in black cotton overalls. Burnishing consisted of rubbing the article with a polished steel tool, or 'burnisher', which had to be kept well lubricated with a soap solution. Finally the article was washed in warm water, dried out in sawdust and rubbed over with a leather. In burnishing, unlike polishing, no metal was removed — the action being to close up the pores of the metal, so producing a polished surface.

Before a product was burnished it was polished on a special lathe with rapidly revolving mops, with various abrasives such as sand, lime or emery being used. It was not a very healthy business and certainly not for weak-chested people, as it was dirty work. After polishing, articles were cleaned by scratch-brushing. This was to free them of any grease which would cause the plated metal to peel off and the process gave a clear bright silken finish to the plated articles. It was done by a circular wire brush on a lathe but was not a popular occupation as the lubrication used made it wet work.

Downstairs in the business was the plating shop, stamp shop and heavy duty shops. Mr Parker was in charge of the soldering shop, staying with the firm until the end. There were many problems with the silveroid production as it was a very hard substance and was hammered ornamentally by hand. Silveroid products were expensive but very long lasting. and sometimes were sent back by customers after having developed a green tinge. This was caused by the products not being used and after a polish they were as good as new, being sent back to customers with the advice: "Use them"!

In the early Twenties there were over one hundred employees in the firm. My mother always used to make the same number of mince pies for the Christmas party and I used to be given, as a child, a huge box of chocolates at this event, although I was more interested in playing on the typewriter. Far fewer people were there in 1931 when I worked there.

To get to work I had to travel on two trams each morning from Kings Heath, where I was living with my Aunt Nellie and Uncle Harry Hitchinson. Out of my £1 a week wages I gave my aunt about six shillings a week and purchased my own meals, so there was little money left over for anything else. I sometimes used to get hot lunches for one shilling from a shop opposite the factory but they were not very nice. I

Typical electro-plated tea services made by the company.

Burnishers at work.

Scratchbrushing.

1925 advertisement in 'Good Housekeeping'.

1912 advertisement.

was always hungry and often filled up on broken biscuits and Mars Bars which were tuppence each.

I spent two years in my father's business, during which time it gradually declined due to the products becoming unfashionable. According to my father it just about paid its way at the end but past debts mounted up which drove the firm to closure in 1935, after twenty years of business. His products never wore out; some teapots and cutlery are still in use in the family today after sixty years which could not have been good for business!

In 1933 I accepted an invitation from my maternal grandparents to live with them for a while in Scarborough. They were concerned at my poor state of health which was probably due to lack of regular nourishment and a proper home, although I did not realise it at the time. It was during my stay that I inherited, at the age of twenty one, a legacy of £1000 from my late mother which was to open up many opportunities in my life.

Typical electro-plating equipment in common use from 1903-30.

Advertisements in Punch, 1932

CHAPTER 4

CHALET FLORA

*"The human flower is the one of all flowers which has most need of sunshine
— therefore send your children where they will get the mountain sun"*, said the
brochure for Chalet Flora School in Switzerland: *"the absence of fog, the
purity and lightness of the air allows health-giving rays of the sun to act
directly upon growing little bodies"* . . .

This glowing description was read by Margo Hitchinson in the autumn of
1934, after answering an advertisement for an 'au-pair student' to teach
English. There was great attention to health in the school where delicate
children of all ages went from all over Europe and beyond, sent by wealthy
parents who could afford the fees. Main lessons were taught in French by
graduate teachers but special lessons were offered in English, which is where
Margo takes up the story, travelling to Switzerland in November 1934:-

I had no real qualifications to teach English except a good Grammar
school education and the 'salary' was the equivalent of about six shillings
(30 p) per week, but I was offered free winter sports which really
attracted me. In those days only the wealthy elite could afford winter
sports so it was a wonderful opportunity. I was determined to see a bit of
the world with my mother's legacy, now that I had come "of age".

I was told that I had to pay my own transport costs which was quite
considerable as it was for a single second class ticket. I was advised to
avoid third class as the hard wooden slatted seats were unbearable in
French railway carriages. £50 today is a derisory figure but in 1934 it was
a very respectable amount. Few people had that sum to fool around with
as life was grim and earnest but it bought adventure for me.

I had to buy some ski trousers and an anorak by post as they were
both unobtainable in Birmingham at that time. Some second-hand ski
boots and a large trunk completed my preparations for the journey.
Friends and relations were either envious or horrified at my decision to go
off into what was rather an unknown world in 1934. My beloved
grandmother tried hard to dissuade me, being fearful for my safety. My
only qualms were about my ability to speak good French but I was told I
would be speaking English most of the time to the pupils.

It was November and "the cross channel steamer seemed to be full of

Gstaad village and skating rink, 1934.

of international crooks'', I wrote back later to my grandmother. Men wore long raincoats and trilby hats in those days and to me they all looked very sinister. They were probably all businessmen and I must have looked very young and innocent to them, travelling solo at the age of twenty one. There was only one other woman on the boat.

On the train from Boulogne the Swiss dawn came with heavy mist but the sun began to shine when I had changed on to the mountain train at Zweissimmen. A man in the same compartment started up a conversation and learned I was going to Gstaad. He roared with laughter when I told him I was going to teach English in a Swiss school. ''You're not a bit like any teacher I ever knew!'', he said. I felt quite offended.

At Gstaad he kindly carried my suitcase and I soon met the schoolmistress who became a future friend. Speaking English perfectly, she tried to put me at ease, looking with slight disapproval at my escort. He raised his hat and hoped I would enjoy my stay in Switzerland. The teacher was past middle age, with rather pain features and anyone could have guessed her profession. He said with a twinkle in his eye before he departed: ''You see what I mean?''. I did!

I looked around at Gstaad which in those days was not so fashionable as today. There was no snow yet but everything was delightfully different. A feeling of excitement gripped me at the thought of the next six months. That adventurous journey, which I would never forget, was over. I had arrived . . .

During those first few days at the school I felt very strange as it was a bit of a nightmare. I hardly caught any of the French that was gabbled at me. As time went on I began to understand more but everyone spoke so fast it was hard work even though I had studied the language at school for four or five years. Some of the teachers spoke no English at all although the headmistress, Madame Winster, had a good command of the language, with a Cockney twang she had learned in London.

The children received an excellent education, together with winter and summer sports amidst magnificent scenery and all nationalities. The day began about 7.30 a.m., when my first job was to dress my room-mate Ray, a little five year old American boy who had forgotten all his native language. He chattered French with an atrocious accent. Breakfast was porridge, followed by brown bread and cheese which was always welcome as everyone had a terrific hunger in the superb mountain air.

Lessons began directly after this meal, lasting about two hours, after which doors opened to disgorge the noisy throng who rushed madly to dress for skiing or skating. They were a cosmopolitan assortment and sometimes hard to manage, especially one uncontrollable Turkish boy who caused many fights and disturbances, giving credence to the saying "a regular little Turk"! I was often heartily glad that I was not a 'proper' school mistress whose task it was to control them.

I had been promised free winter sports but they had not mentioned that it was to be my task every morning to put on all those little skating boots belonging to the 'tinies', before we set off for the ice rink in the village. After this chore, I was free to perform on the ice myself. I soon found my skating legs as I had done some roller skating but inevitably had several hard falls before I finally began to move rhythmically. Then it was time to take off all those little boots again! . . .

The same thing more or less happened in the afternoon when we were skiing. I had to labour to get all those small children equipped and dressed for the snow and eventually push them off. They were far more expert than myself and seemed to have been born with a supreme sense of balance, while I bumbled along like a ponderous mountain bear. The sports mistress gave all her instructions in French and I soon gave up trying to understand it.

As the winter and my ski-ing progressed we sometimes had a mountain picnic during ski-ing sessions. The lunch was taken up to the Bissen, a small hill not far away where there was a farm belonging to the Chalet. The hot mountain meal, including soup, was served in the sunshine which was most enjoyable.

There were other lessons, of course, and I was officially known as the English teacher — Miss Margot. Ray got the name wrong and called me 'Escargot' instead; he must have seen my progress on the ski slopes! I had little free time and marvel now how I got through the timetable. To nine different children — Belgian, Italian, American, Swiss and Egyptian

Skiing excursion from Chalet Flora.

— I taught English grammar, dictation and composition as well as arithmetic, reading and translation. As I had no formal qualifications it was quite a formidable task. Two teenage Egyptian girls knew almost as much English as I did. When we read the classics together words I had never heard of would sometimes crop up. I would suggest that the girls looked them up in a dictionary so that they would remember them better — it was a battle of wits!

At lunch time there was a scramble by the children to reach 'Tante Flora', the headmistress, as she was beloved by all. Everyone ate heartily after the exercise of the morning, after which there was a 'siesta' for an hour and a half, when all children were compelled to lie down to rest. I dreaded having to take my turn to take charge of the siesta two or three times a week. I had no experience at maintaining discipline and some of the little terrors used to go off into shrieks of laughter at my inadequate French.

Skiing followed until tea-time, a joyous proceeding in which the children revelled in throwing themselves with abandon down the nursery slopes near the school, often tumbling head-first into depths of soft powdery snow amid shrieks of laughter. Afterwards, there was the labour of getting them into a fit condition for tea, which was a scant meal taken in a hurry. Lessons followed again until supper and bed-time.

At Christmas I was asked to produce Charles Dickens' "Christmas

Carol'', the Cratchit scene, for a group of parents visiting the chalet at the end of term. Despite protesting that the children did not know enough English, the play went ahead with a most unlikely cast. I was in charge although I was only an 'au pair' and had no training whatsoever in teaching or drama!

It was a headache from start to finish and I cannot really believe I ever managed it all, but the great day arrived. I was introduced to the parents as the English teacher and we began our little show. I doubt if anyone back home would have recognised the text, so peculiar were the accents. I was the only English person present who could appreciate that distorted Dickensian dialogue! To my surprise the parents liked the play and I was congratulated on a good effort. Whether Charles Dickens would have recognized his masterpiece is another matter!

I left the school after six months and many years later I returned to Gstaad which had developed into an expensive and exclusive resort with ski hoists and cable cars galore. I couldn't help gloating that once I had plodded up the Hornberg before they existed, on my own two skis, for absolutely nothing — or should I say six shillings a week!

La Propriété du Chalet Flora

(70 000 m²)

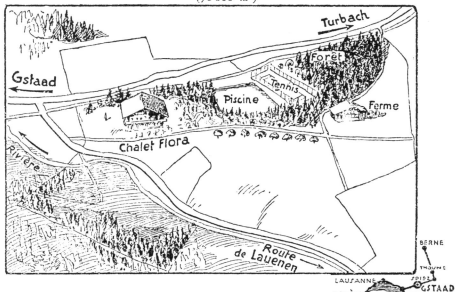

CHAPTER 5

RISING DREAMS

On her return to England in 1935 Margo Hitchinson felt she should make the most of her inheritance as her travels had widened her horizons. She resumed living in Scarbororough with her grandparents who offered her a permanent home. Her plans for the future were very vague and uncertain until one day she saw an advertisement which gave her an idea, as she narrates:-

It really began in the library. I had been looking at some magazines when an advertisement caught my eye: "WANTED. Two girls as apprentice cake makers. Live in. Pocket money only until trained. Apply: The Olde Malte Tea House, Amersham, Bucks".

Perhaps I am impulsive but I knew the advertisement was exactly what I was seeking. My head seemed to whirl with all sorts of plans for the future as I enjoyed cooking in my grandmother's kitchen. Maybe I could even open a home-made cake shop when I had learned a few things! . . .

I sent off a letter immediately and had a reply by return of post. I was rather horrified to learn that the 'pocket money' offered was only 2/6d. weekly for the first month, then 5/- until they thought I was worth more. Even in those hard times it seemed like slave labour! However, board and lodging was free and I would get half a day off each week, with the promise of a two-day weekend every month.

My gentle grandmother had distinct doubts about my sudden proposed flight from her household but she knew me well enough not to stop me. I had been to Switzerland come to no harm. My grandfather saw me off at the busy station the following Sunday. We did not talk much as we walked along but I felt the old man was not unsympathetic. When he had got me settled into the carriage he gave me a long hard look with his faded cornflower-blue eyes. The most sentimental of men, he hid his true feelings under a rather brusque exterior.

"You may not like it much when you get there", he said drily, "but try to stick it out. If you find it quite unbearable you know you can always come back here." Then he paused. "I hate goodbyes so I won't stop" — and he was was gone with never a backward glance. I felt quite choked with emotion for a moment and could almost have shed a tear but it was good to know that I could always come back to Scarborough.

It made me all the more determined than ever not to return with my tail between my legs.

As the train gathered speed I was beset with doubts and I gazed unseeingly out of the window. It had been a happy life with my grandparents but I had little money without employment and you cannot vegetate when you are twenty two years old. I wanted desperately to find something financially rewarding for the small amount of capital I had from my mother's legacy. Anyway, it was fun to be travelling by train again, with the wonderful expectancy of adventure . . .

I arrived at the Olde Malte Tea House in Amersham in the afternoon when everyone there seemed very busy as over three hundred teas were often served on a Sunday. It was an impressive old building with genuine oak beams and small windows all over the place. Originally it had been a barn and had been converted with the cafe on the upper floor.

Later on I met the other girls. There were two cake-makers, Yvonne and Jane, both of whom had passed an apprenticeship in their art, and a young Irish girl apprentice. The two middle-aged spinsters who owned the place were very efficient. One was in charge of the bakery while the other looked after the catering side of the business. The Olde Malte Tea House was very striking, the tremendous oak beams giving the 'olde worlde' atmosphere. The food served in the cafe was excellent so it was a favourite place for Londoners to go in the Thirties, being a pleasant drive by car.

I knew I had a lot to learn and worked hard, keeping secret my ultimate goal which I imparted to no-one. I was soon making huge bowls of Victoria sandwich mixture by hand which was the practice in those days in similar establishments. We literally got our hands in it, being told that the warmth of our hands would help to cream the mixture.

We never stopped working and always felt tired. It was sheer bliss to lie

down on our beds at night to rest our weary
bodies and just talk. We were four attractive
girls with no hope of a boyfriend between us
as we never had time to meet any!

The first baking of the day was the bread
which we put in the bakery ovens downstairs,
before we had our breakfast upstairs in a
room overlooking the tiny garden. Sometimes the bread was ready before
we had finished our meal and someone had to check if it was fully
cooked, usually the two apprentices. A loaf is fully baked when it sounds
hollow but more often than not I was never very sure so I had a brilliant
idea, devising a quick way of finding out. I persuaded Yvonne and Jane,
our experts, to open the window and to catch one loaf which I threw up
from the garden near the bakery. I was good at catching things . . . but
they were not! It caused great hilarity and noise when a practically red
hot loaf came zooming up . . . especially when they missed it! Breakfast
time became something to look forward to but, alas, our fun and games
came to a sudden end when the owners of the establishment found out!

One day I had some visitors from Worcester — the Price family, with
whom I had spent many happy holidays as a child, after my mother's
death. Mrs Price was very forthright, telling me that I had lost a lot of
weight and must be working too hard as I did not look well. A letter
came a few days later from the owners of a Worcester bakery who knew
Mrs Price, offering me a job with much higher wages. I felt it would be a
good opportunity to learn how another business was conducted so I left
the Olde Malte Tea House after four months hard work. I told them of
my hopes for the future and we vowed to meet again. Sadly, we never
did . . .

My new employers lived in a tiny cottage at Spetchley, five miles from
Worcester,the bakery being at the back. They needed more help as they
were opening a shop in Worcester. The worst job in the bakery was to
clean the ovens which ran on oil. This had to be done every Monday
morning and was hardly a pleasant duty as there was a certain
accumulation of grease to be removed. I was surprised to see how well
this type of oven cooked the cakes. Cake recipes were quite different
from the ones I had been taught previously and I had to help sell the
cakes once a week in the Worcester shop.

Transport to the town was an old bicycle, which I enjoyed at first until
the nights became darker in the autumn. It was eerie to cycle along five
miles of mostly pitch black country roads and it was also extremely tiring.
I managed to buy a cheap motor cycle which cost £5 — and was sold two
years later for £4.17.6d! The Excelsior two-stroke machine only needed
one gallon for about 100 miles but it had its limitations, especially going
up hills. It was not very pleasant in the winter weather when I had to
wear my old voluminous ski trousers. Snow was distinctly unpleasant,

DOWN ON THE FARM—
OR IN ANY HOME

Modernise your kitchen with a Valor-Perfection Oil Cooking Stove and forget your coal worries. Do away with all dust, dirt, and trouble. A woman's stove made as she would make it. Everything in sight and within easy reach. Easy to light. Clean and movable. No guess work—you know because you can see the progress of the cooking through the glass door of the oven. Don't cook in the dark—cook in the light and right way on a

VALOR-PERFECTION
Oil Cooking Stove

Good Housekeeping advertisement, 1922.

even though I wore a white leather helmet, as the flakes felt like lead shot against my face. But my motor cycle was priceless to me at that time, a means of cheap transport when I was earning very little money.

I had a little more social life now and joined a badminton club. I remember at the time that everyone discussed the news of the King and Mrs Simpson. I sometimes went to Birmingham to visit friends and on one of my visits I met the mother of my old school friend, Ethel Baldwin. When I told her that I was hoping eventually to open a shop on the outskirts of Birmingham she said Ethel was looking for work. There was even the suggestion that Ethel might be interested in joining me in my venture as a partner. Suddenly, it seemed as if my dreams for the future could become a reality . . .

Advertisement in Birmingham Gazette, 1932.

BAKERS RISE TO FAME

The baker here has not risen stolidly—that is just as it should be. You see British D.C.L. Yeast has done its good work thoroughly, and the dough is silky and buoyant . . . just in the right condition for the heat of the oven to transform it into beautiful, golden-brown loaves. You, too, can rise to the top if you let British D.C.L.—IN ONE POUND PACKETS—do the rising part of your baking.

ON **DCL**

THE PROFITABLE YEAST

The UNITED YEAST Co. Ltd., MANCHESTER, BIRMINGHAM, BRISTOL, LEEDS, LONDON, NEWCASTLE-ON-TYNE

CHAPTER 6

THE RISE OF "4 O'CLOCK"

'Hitchinson and Baldwin' came to life in 1936, a partnership formed between Margo Hitchinson and Ethel Baldwin for a project tackled with much enthusiasm and very few assets.

Ethel Baldwin had not the same mixed experience as her partner but had been a cookery demonstrator for the firm of Triplex Grates and a tea promoter for the Ceylon Tea Company. What she lacked in experience she made up with great enthusiasm and zeal for their proposed business, as she narrates:-

> I was sure that this was what I wanted to do although my father was
> filled with misgivings. But to me it seemed to be so right at the time and
> I felt a driving force to carry on with the idea of starting up a cake shop
> and cafe.

Margo thought Ethel's enthusiasm would be a great asset, as she relates:-

> I felt that Ethel's company would make the whole thing more
> pleasurable, even though I wondered how she would react to the sheer
> messiness of cooking. I had no illusions that it would be extremely hard
> work for very little gain, especially at first. Many people thought us crazy
> to be attempting to start up a business with so little capital, especially in
> those hard times. We started with a capital of only £50. I used £25 of my
> legacy and Ethel borrowed £25 from her mother, so the whole business
> certainly started on a shoe-string.
>
> We started looking around for suitable premises and soon found it was
> not going to be an easy task to find the right property at the right price.
> The shop we liked the best was on the Yardley Road in Acocks Green
> which had a reasonable rent. It was a modern shop with living
> accommodation and was just past 'Harold's Garage', a cycle shop and
> garage, opposite Cottesbrook Road. We knew we could not afford to live
> in the flat above the shop and proposed to take out only £1 each per
> week, as wages, when we started.
>
> The shop had been a delicatessen business which had failed so we
> thought that the agent would be pleased to have our offer. However, he
> seemed to view us with horror, indicating that our youth, (we were both

View of Yardley Road shops, from Douglas Road to Harold's Garage, 1934.
(J. Marks)

twenty three at the time), was the greatest impediment. When he learned that we intended to sub-let the flat, it was the final straw and we made no progress, despite Ethel turning on her considerable charm. After this setback we despondently continued to look for other shops during the next few weeks but found nothing as good at the right price. One day, travelling by bus, we passed by this previous mecca of our hopes and saw that the shop was still empty and forlorn. We decided to tackle the agent once again as he had obviously been unable to let the property.

The agent seemed to relent a little when we pointed out he was losing money on the property but he demanded guarantors in case we failed and suggested our fathers. This was quite impossible as mine had recently become bankrupt and Ethel's father still had several children at school to support. After a battle with himself, the agent suddenly made up his mind and accepted our offer, so we quickly left before he changed his mind.

Jubilantly we made some plans and Ethel contacted two Welsh school teachers who wanted to occupy the flat. My accommodation problem was solved when an old family friend, Mrs Phillips, came to the rescue. She lived a few doors away from my father and step-mother in Nansen Road.

We started to spend our capital of £50, using a large proportion of it to re-wire the flat so that the electricity supply was separate from the shop. We purchased some lino for the shop floor and made do with bare boards in the room beyond which was to be the bakery. We managed to

buy from the Gas showrooms a large second-hand oven which did splendid service for a great many years. The previous owner sold us the counter for ten shillings and we dressed it up in chinz at one shilling a yard. We were also offered all the shelving but we refused and ripped it all out with gay abandon, which we were to regret later during the war.

I had wonderful ideas of the 'olde worlde' look of the Olde Malte Tea House at the back of my mind. We purchased, with our rapidly disappearing capital, an imitation antique plate rack to hang on the wall to give this impression. Chairs and tables came mostly from my grandparents in Scarborough who had said that I could have anything I could find in their attic. The tables were rather rickety but all the items I found travelled down to Birmingham by rail for next to nothing.

We positioned the tables and chairs on the left hand side of the shop, to create 'the cafe'. The right hand side of the shop was to be solely for the sale and display of cakes, scones and bread. A screen divided the two parts and the door was in the middle of the two bay windows. In the windows we displayed cakes and pastries on one side and jams, marmalades, lemon and orange curd on the other. This latter idea was Ethel's and it proved to be a good sales stand-by. It was also easy to make jams in the right season when business was slack.

Ethel recounts her memories of setting up the shop:-

I bought some antique shelves at a little shop in Sparkhill which I had known since my childhood. We had the counter reversed so that it was an 'L' shape which gave an open space in the shop. This meant we were in contact with our customers which made for an informal and friendly atmosphere.

Before we opened I began making jams and marmalades at home to sell in the shop. I collected from various sources anything and everything which would be useful. An aunt who was moving house gave us a large kitchen table and numerous cooking and kitchen utensils.

I used to set out from home loaded down with bags, making a very different picture from the elegant gloved and hatted young woman I had previously been. I used to baulk at carrying anything other than a matching handbag but all that went out of the window when I had my teeth into the project! Nothing would stop me! To reach the shop from home I could have travelled on two buses but I was so short of money that I often used to catch the No. 1A bus to Acocks Green village and then walked up the Yardley Road to the shop. When we opened a

View of '4 o'Clock' on the Yardley Road, in the row of shops near Harold's Garage in 1936. (K. Aitken)

working day could consist of nine hours standing or walking — no wonder I developed arthritic hips later on!

Margo explains how they named their shop:-

For a long time we could not think of a good name for our business. Then one happy day Ethel had a brainwave. "What about 4 o'Clock?" she said hesitantly. "That's it!" I said immediately, "It's exactly right . . . unusual and it implies everything for afternoon tea!". She was rather astonished at my enthusiasm but as soon as she had said it I knew it was right. We spent some of our dwindling money on a hanging sign for the pavement just outside, to draw attention to the business. It was almost extravagant to have the sign made, considering the state of our finances, but it helped to finalize our brain child and very proud we were of it.

Friends and relations had done their best to help us open the shop. A bank clerk devised a foolproof and easy method of book-keeping which proved very satisfactory. Several friends presented us with odd articles and one even brought a rambler rose on his bicycle to enhance the garden at the back. Ethel's numerous boy friends proved invaluable in their help and one in the electrical business fixed us up with some splendid lights which hung on chains from the ceiling.

It only remained for us to stock up with raw materials from a

"4 o'Clock" cafe and cake-shop at 73 Yardley Road, Acocks Green. (E. Farrow)

wholesaler and to arrange a regular supply of yeast to be delivered. We had decided to make an oven full of bread each day — twelve loaves. There was little profit in this and it kept the oven occupied too long in the morning but we both knew that home-made bread is a great attraction to most people. We hoped to tempt them with other things. The smell of fresh bread cooking was always one of the great assets of "4 o'Clock". People loved the delicious aromas when they walked in and bought more than they intended.

I am sure we were a source of wonder to our fellow shop-keepers. Harold Cheshire, the neighbouring garage proprietor who later became a friend, says his first impression was of two girls sitting on the counter swinging their legs. He became a regular customer and even drove Ethel in his car on one occasion, to deliver a large number of Christmas cakes to Sparkhill. Transport was always a problem for delivery of cake orders and we used to depend on friends helping us with their cars.

By the time we got to "opening day" there was little money left in the kitty but we had our stock of raw materials and the two teachers were installed in the flat. For this important day of our lives we advertised with printed leaflets and were very busy indeed that first day, taking several pounds in money. Cakes and pastries, which were inexpensive in those days, sold for the following prices :

Bread	3d. per loaf
Scones	5 for 3d.
Rock cakes	4 for 3d.
Victoria sponges	8d. and 1/-
Plain cakes	1d. or 1½d.

We also made larger varieties of cakes and a lot of fruit pies and other pastries. The latter was Ethel's idea as she thought suburban housewives would be likely to buy these for their families as an easy pudding. She was proved right.

We were delighted with the interest we were causing on that first day and during one of the busy periods Ethel popped her head round the door into the back room, where I was working, to chortle: "Guess who's in here?". "Who?", I said, mystified. "It's Mr Bickley from the Estate Agents. He's busy choosing some cakes to take to his wife!". This was splendid news as the Agents had probably sent him to give us the 'once over', and I like to think that he was relieved by what he saw in the shop.

Between us we found we could tackle most things and I took on the book-keeping and the ordering of supplies. Both of us could make the varieties of cakes we had decided to sell although we each had our own specialities. I was better at icing cakes whereas Ethel was a better pastry-cook. Between us we had a fund of ideas and we were always looking for new recipes.

My partner stood up well to the messiness of cooking although she did not approve of me using my hands to make large quantities of mixture and preferred a wooden spoon. I soon found I had to abandon my method as we sometimes had to break off our labours to serve in the shop and getting rid of a lot of sticky mixture from your hands in a few seconds could not be done!

Some favourite cakes were sticky current buns, green marzipan cakes shaped like lettuces and Maids of Honour which were puff pastry, filled with a mixture of egg, caster sugar and ground almonds. Other popular cakes included iced Sponge Fingers filled with jam and Nut Browns which were made of eggs and caster sugar whipped together, with raisins, dates and walnuts.

Ethel remembers the cakes they used to make:-

Every morning we made a batch of rock cakes and scones. Typical recipes were:-

Rock cakes — 8 oz S.R. flour, 4oz margarine, 4oz demerara sugar, pinch of salt, 4 oz mixed fruit and peel.

Scones — 1 lb flour, 4 oz lard/margarine, 3 oz sugar, 3 oz dried fruit

We had a regular customer for jam tarts. A large Staffordshire bull terrier used to come over the road each morning, from a shop opposite our business, for a jam tart and he would only accept a fresh one! The Yardley Road was not so busy with traffic in those days.

At the end of each day there would be an enormous pile of dirty bowls, basins, tins and wooden spoons waiting to be washed up, as Margo recalls:-

We advertised for a lady for cleaning duties and Mrs Snelson joined our establishment. She cleaned our premises once a week and made the lino in the shop shine so much we were afraid our customers would slip and break their necks! Over the years her efforts were beyond price and her loyalty beyond question. She relished relating the "goings-on" of her family which caused us much amusement but often infuriated us by arriving late to do the washing-up. However, she never failed to turn up without a wonderful excuse and every time we saw her we were always so relieved, knowing we should not have to tackle the job ourselves, that we willingly forgave her.

The brisk business of our first day did not last but we settled down to a steady trickle of customers, many of whom became regulars. Several travelled quite a distance to buy our home-made bread. If our takings were about £1 daily we thought we were doing quite well. On Fridays and Saturdays we made much more but some days we sold very little. The great enemy was waste and we used to examine the cakes every day to see if we dare put them in the window again. Ethel's mother had a huge bag full on Saturday nights at rock bottom prices for her large family. This was invaluable and prevented them from being completely wasted.

After six months trading we had the bill for the rates. To pay it would have taken every penny we had so we hung on as long as we dared. Eventually we had to settle it and from that date our business improved and our income increased.

Grif and Gil, our two school teachers in the flat, got us an order for several mince pies at 1d. each, for their Christmas party so we worked late one night getting these baked. The Christmas trade was very helpful and our customers were beginning to know us well enough to give us orders for traditional cakes. Slowly our takings grew although we were still only paying ourselves £1 per week.

For some time the cafe part of the shop was not very busy, apart from the odd traveller and housewife coming in for a cup of tea. By 1937 we were slowly getting busier. For Coronation Day we celebrated by making three Victoria sponges in patriotic colours, one of which sold immediately but the others hung fire for ages. In the end we cut up one to sell as pieces of cake and the other was used in a manner I had learned in my apprenticeships. There are several tricks of the trade where cakes can be made out of old sponge mixture with the addition of ground almonds,

apricot jam and a little ingenuity. The following Christmas was quite busy and from then on we never looked like failing. We began to take a living wage out of the business.

Several of our friends were getting married and we were entrusted with making and icing some wedding cakes. The icing was a great responsibility as I had never learned this art. As I was generally invited to the wedding receptions of these friends I felt like having a heart attack when the cakes were cut, in case of a disaster! Once we catered for a whole buffet reception for a school friend which involved a lot of transportation of food in Ethel's boyfriend's car. We were hostesses on this important day and were pleased when it was declared a resounding success as well as being highly profitable for us. It was unfortunate for me that my best friend Joan was married on that same day so I was only able to visit her reception for a few minutes.

I had to find alternative lodgings in 1938 as my friends, Mr and Mrs Phillips, were leaving Birmingham. Mrs Phillips had been practically a mother to me so it was a great blow. However I found a pleasant place where I had bed and breakfast and Sunday meals, and I ate the rest of the time at the shop. The shop became more than my working place, almost my headquarters.

Life was beginning to be very pleasant when Chamberlain's visit to Munich in 1938 brought everyone to a horrifying halt. Whatever was happening in Europe? Could we be on the brink of war? We were as pleased as anyone to welcome his "peace in our time" but these events had left a canker in the bud of our smug existence and we were never to be so carefree again.

The outbreak of war in September 1939 seemed unbelievable. Our future now seemed so uncertain although trade was brisk. We had begun to know our customers very well in those bleak years of the Depression which effected everyone. We were lucky to have employment in the Thirties when jobs were scarce and poorly paid. We were always aware that we were serving working people who had very little spare cash for such luxuries as cakes.

Our three years had been so challenging, with many hours of hard work and very little financial reward — but thoroughly enjoyable! We felt that we had triumphed through our own efforts. At least we had the satisfaction of knowing we had started a business, against all odds, which could now be considered to be a success. What would the future bring? . . .

CHAPTER 7

WARTIME AT "4 O'CLOCK"

On Sunday 3rd September 1939 the Prime Minister, Mr Neville Chamberlain, announced on the radio that a state of war existed between Great Britain and Germany. At that time Margo Hitchinson was at the Malvern Tennis Club playing a Ladies Singles Final and saw a silvery barrage balloon rise majestically into the blue sky. She recalls the moment:-

We stopped playing and there was some nervous joking. We were at war! It was a very solemn and terrible moment when the sirens suddenly began to wail, the first of our false alarms.

As everyone knows, those first few months of the war were known as the 'phoney war'. A lot of organisation went on for fire-watching and the A.R.P. (Air Raid Precautions) came into being. The sirens sounded a note of terror as they rose and fell until the long continuous note gave the 'all clear'.

Gas masks were issued to everyone and had to be carried at all times. Special ones were made for babies and children under four years old were given a Mickey Mouse mask to make them seem less repellent. Even cart-horses and dogs could be fitted with masks in case of gas bombs.

Blackout curtains were the order of the day as all lights had to be extinguished to deter enemy aircraft above Birmingham. Supplies soon ran out of blackout material and torches, causing the first war shortages. To reduce accidents most permanent obstructions, such as lamp posts and kerbs, were given bands of white paint and cars also had markings on bumpers and running boards.

Anderson shelters were delivered and had to be constructed in back gardens at a depth of 4 feet. They were designed to withstand a 500 pound bomb falling 20 feet away but were difficult to erect and often damp. Newspapers were full of tips to make these air raid shelters more comfortable. One article recommended heating a brick in the oven and rolling a blanket around it to keep a body warm in bed! Many people were destined in the next few years to huddle in terror in their shelters in dim candlelight, listening to the drone of enemy aircraft and the sound of falling bombs.

To make things seem worse, the B.B.C. shut down all radio channels

*Another use for
the gas mask!*
(Landworker,
1940).

National Identity card.

except the Home Service. Even theatres and cinemas closed, although they soon re-opened again to provide a welcome release from the tension of the war effort. No-one could move around without carrying their National Registration card which was even issued to children.

The local R.A.F. personnel on the Barrage Balloon site found our shop and cafe as a source of sustinence as they had no canteen at first. They arrived just at the wrong time, when we were hoping to have a quiet dinner hour. However, we were glad of the custom and did our best to produce some lunch when we knew they were coming. They were a cheerful lot, full of good humoured banter and were delighted to have found two feminine shop-keepers to feed them. One used to amble up to the door of our bakery back room, look in and say lazily, "Now, what about some pud?!" Needless to say, he got what we could supply!

We had other R.A.F. visitors too. About ten men from the Polish Air Force, billeted on the Yardley Road, used to come every morning for tea or coffee. Ethel's brother was a navigator in bombers and he sometimes brought friends when they were all on leave. My tennis friends would also drop in so our little bakery became quite a meeting place for young people. Although we enjoyed the company and there was much fun and laughter, it was sometimes disconcerting to be watched whilst making cakes as we couldn't afford to make mistakes.

Food rationing began in 1940 for basic foods such as meat, sugar, butter, eggs and cheese. Ration books were distributed and everyone had to register with a grocer and butcher. There was great excitement when shops had little extras and word would go round like wildfire when bananas, oranges or tomatoes appeared. People would queue for hours for just one of each. An average weekly ration for each person included 8 oz sugar, 4 oz butter, 1 oz cheese, and 1 egg, although it varied during the war how much was rationed.

Permits had to be obtained from the government for the raw materials we used in the shop. We filled in many forms about how much sugar, fat, flour, fruit and other things we had used in 1939. Flour was purchased from Mr Townsend of the A1 Flour Company in Sparkbrook. Two travelling salesmen, who called once a month at our shop for orders, gave us a great deal of help in filling in the forms. When the permits arrived they were quite generous for a shop of our size and I always suspected that we had more sugar than we should have done. This meant that our cakes were often sweeter than those from other establishments. We made the most of our generous supply of raw materials by selling some on the black market so we had very regular and faithful customers!

"4 o'Clock" in wartime.

We had never attempted to compete with the larger bakeries by making cream cakes such as eclairs and cream buns. Now that other bakeries were unable to make such cakes our home-made cakes were more popular than ever, especially as they were sweeter than those in other shops.

Tinned food also began to be in short supply, especially as the war progressed and the convoys were decimated. We had always carried a small stock of tinned food, mostly luxury items, but now Ethel suggested that we bought all we could lay our hands on, as an investment for the future. At first, I demurred, not wanting to turn our attractive shop into a grocers: but the situation was now entirely different and it would take all our ingenuity to survive. We now regretted we had taken down the shop shelves when we first opened as we had to put up new ones for our stock of tins. The regular travellers who called were always very kind, perhaps because we were a couple of girls, and helped us to obtain tinned goods. The tins soon sold as shelves and pantries everywhere were becoming very empty.

Margo Hitchinson.

Eggs were our biggest headache during the war, as they couldn't be obtained anywhere. At first we used cheap shell eggs which we used to buy in crates. They were imported from China or Europe, costing about 1d. an egg, but this source of supply soon dried up. Unlike the established bakers we had never used tinned eggs so we were not allowed any on permit.

"I want a dozen egg-cups, please — and do you know where I can get some eggs?"
(Punch, 1941)

When the first cargo of dried egg arrived from America it was rationed to one packet per person every four weeks. A packet was the equivalent of twelve eggs. We found American 'Lend/Lease' dried egg quite good when we got used to it but even this was sometimes difficult to obtain in the later stages of the war. We pleaded with all sorts of people for cracked eggs and often resorted to recipes which were egg-less. We had a lucky break in finding someone at a Badminton club who produced eggs in a big way. In return for somewhat preferential treatment for our cakes he supplied us with most of his damaged eggs. We also found someone else with a chicken farm who supplied us with two or three dozen eggs each week, in exchange for butter and sugar.

"DRIED EGGS are my eggs – my whole eggs and nothing but my eggs"

Dried eggs are the complete hen's eggs, both the white and the yolk, dried to a powder. Nothing is added. Nothing but moisture and the shell taken away, leaving the eggs themselves as wholesome, as digestible and as full of nourishment and health-protecting value as if you had just taken the eggs new laid from the nest. So put the eggs back into your breakfast menus. And what about a big, creamy omelette for supper? You can have it savoury; or sweet, now that you get extra jam.

DRIED EGGS build you up!

In war-time, the most difficult foods for us to get are the body-builders. Dried eggs build muscle and repair tissue in just the same way as do chops and steaks; and are better for health-protection. So we are particularly lucky to be able to get dried eggs to make up for any shortage of other body-builders such as meat, fish, cheese, milk.

Your allowance of DRIED EGG is equal to 3 eggs a week

You can now get one 12-egg packet (price 1 3) per 4-week rationing period — three fine fresh eggs a week, at the astonishingly low price of

1¼d. each. Children (holders of green ration books) get two packets each rationing period. You buy your dried eggs at the shop where you are registered for shell eggs; poultry keepers can buy anywhere.

Don't hoard your dried eggs; use them up — there are plenty more coming!

Note. *Don't make up dried eggs until you are ready to use them; they should not be allowed to stand after they've been mixed with water or other liquid. Use dry when making cakes and so on, and add a little more moisture when mixing.*

FREE — DRIED EGG LEAFLET containing many interesting recipes, will be sent on receipt of a postcard addressed to Dept. 627E, Food Advice Service, Ministry of Food, London, W.1.

ISSUED BY THE MINISTRY OF FOOD   (S.74)

A wartime advertisement for egg powder.

In April 1940 Ethel Baldwin married Leonard Farrow, who was a gunner in the Royal Engineers, as she recalls:-

I first went out with Len Farrow on Coronation Day in 1937 but was too engrossed in "4 o'Clock" to spare much time for him! It's a wonder he persisted but he used to come to the shop on Saturday nights when it was my turn keep open until 9 p.m. He always offered to buy the remaining cakes and also offered to buy me clothes as I was very short of money during the first years of our venture. I utterly refused to allow him to buy me anything as I felt it was one of the first signs of being a kept woman in those days! However, after my home in Sparkhill was bombed in 1940 I went to live with Mrs Farrow, as all my family was either evacuated or enlisted in the forces. This led to our engagement.

Ethel & Leonard Farrow's wedding, April 1940.

Margo recalls that she had been going out with several boyfriends from the tennis club:-

There was one attentive young man in whose car we enjoyed long rides into the countryside but petrol rationing put an end to these pleasant

Let Dr Carrot protect you

"Call me in often enough, and you'll keep well," says Dr. Carrot. Vitamin A is essential to good health ; and carrots are one of its richest sources. Thanks to the British farmer there's a grand crop.

excursions. He was in the catering business and once demonstrated his art in decorating cakes by icing a birthday cake we had on order. He had been properly trained so iced it beautifully but also had a cigarette dangling from his mouth all the time he worked. I was terrified that the ash would fall on the cake! He suddenly got bored and finished the sides of the cake in a very slip-shod fashion which I later scraped off and finished in my own hand.

When he came to call for me on another evening the cake was still there and, of course, he saw that the top of it was his handiwork and the rest mine! He looked at me and said drily, "That's the last cake I shall do for you!"

There was also someone else who was often around, especially after I had caught the measles and was ill on my own in my digs. Maurice Headford very kindly came in during his lunch hour to 'feed and water' me for which I was extremely grateful. He worked at Charles Churchill Machine Tools Company, near the Swan in South Yardley. He was also in digs as his home town was Maidstone and was a fellow member of Malvern Tennis Club.

On the 29th May 1940 we became engaged on my birthday and decided to marry in August. The flat above the shop had just become vacant so there seemed no point in waiting as we were both anxious for a home in those awful days when the Battle of Britain was beginning. Maurice was in no danger of being called up as he was an engineering draughtsman in the machine tool industry.

Air raids were just starting to take place but were "nuisance raids" rather than the blitzes which came later. I treated them rather lightly at first until one night I had to spend a few lonely hours in the broom cupboard at my lodgings in Kilmorrie Road. Everyone else had gone to a shelter but I had gone to bed earlier. My nerves were never the same again after that experience and I was always glad of the protection of those wonderful shelters in the future.

The few weeks leading up to our wedding were very hectic as I had to run the shop on my own as Ethel was ill. We were also trying to furnish

A chocolate cake...   *A cocktail and a half...*   *less than 50 cigarettes...*

A bunch of flowers, if you're lucky...

TWO-AND-SIXPENCE! That's the new price of Vogue. With Vogue Pattern Book, of course.

A bit of a wrench—parting with half a crown—these difficult days? We know it. We didn't want to put the price up, but soaring costs forced us to. But just consider. . . .

Consider how lightly you spend half a crown on a few hours' pleasure, or less. Consider that when you buy Vogue you get a month's value, or more. Every Vogue now is a Double Number. Vogue itself—packed with exciting features and helpful ideas. Vogue Pattern Book—packed with smart designs for dressmaking. Here are real fashion news, clothes from the shops, economy ideas, beauty, patterns, good reading, fine photographs—for less than you pay for a cinema seat or a chocolate cake!

A seat at the local flicks...

Half a pair of stockings...

So don't be extravagant—and cut down on your Vogue. You can't afford to! The two-and-six it costs can save you pounds—mis-spent on clothes which " date " or don't pull their weight in your wardrobe.

Talking of value . . . you'll find the next Vogue a gilt-edged investment. The Beauty and Younger Generation Number. Packed with war-time beauty, children's clothes and news, holiday clothes and looks, advance Autumn fashions. It's due on July 24: price 2/6, with Vogue Pattern Book. But you *must* order it *now*, or you may not get it.

A gallon and a drop of petrol...

VOGUE with VOGUE PATTERN BOOK · PRICE 2'6 →

or two money-saving magazines!

Some examples of what you could by for half a crown in 1940, including a seat at the flicks or a gallon of petrol! (Vogue, July 1940).

the flat where we would live after our marriage. On many an evening we had to retire to the Anderson shelter during air raids so I lost a lot of sleep as well as weight in that time. Somehow I managed to slap a wedding cake together, resenting every minute of the precious time it took me to ice it, as I had so many other things to do.

A few days before our wedding some big bombs fell on the city centre and in Sparkhill not far away. There were time bombs outside several Birmingham shops, including the one where I had ordered my wedding hat. At another shop was our bed on order so I began to wonder what Fate had in store for us in the future . . .

..*Shoot straight, Lady*

The drive to Victory — part of a government advertisement aimed at womens' war efforts.

You've got a fighting job on hand, too. These are significant days and anyone — man, woman, or child — who is less than fighting fit is a pull back on the total war effort.

FOOD is your munition of war. The Government sees that you get the right stuff and it's vital that you should know how to use it to full advantage . . .

There's cheese : it makes muscle and bone.

There are potatoes : they give energy and warmth.

Carrots, that give vitality and help you to see in the dark.

Green vegetables, with their valuable salts and vitamins, which are so very important for clear complexions and sound teeth.

CHAPTER 8

LIFE DURING THE BLITZ AT "4 O'CLOCK"

Gas masks were carried by all the guests at Margo Hitchinson's wedding. She was married to Maurice Headford on the 31st August 1940 at St Christopher's church in Sparkhill, after having lost over a stone in weight in the weeks leading up to the event.

Her grandparents were unable to to travel down from Yorkshire but Margaret Southwell sent a very welcoming letter to Maurice, in which she admitted that Margo had always been her favourite grandchild. Margo was destined to see her grandparents only once again as Thomas Southwell died shortly after her wedding and her grandmother the following year. They are commemorated in Thwing church with a beautiful stained glass window.

Margo reminisces on her wedding:-

No-one wore traditional white dresses in wartime so I had chosen a pretty coat and dress, only to find I could not collect the matching hat as it was marooned in a Birmingham shop which had closed because of a time-bomb outside the premises. At the very last minute it re-opened so I did just manage to get it in time for the ceremony! The bed which was on order for the flat was not available until weeks later so we had to make do without it.

The weather was glorious on my wedding day as was so much of that wonderful summer of 1940 but no-one was in the mood for frivolities. My husband's parents managed to come up by train from Kent but were anxious to return home again as soon as possible. The reception was held at a friend's house and was a very informal affair. My father later wrote to my grandmother: "The guests did not talk about the usual things at a reception but were eager to swap the latest in bomb stories!"

We spent our honeymoon in the country in leafy Warwickshire, staying at a farmhouse we knew by the River Avon. Every night we heard the bombers making their way to some planned destination, no doubt finding the river useful for navigation. We knew that Birmingham was the target but did not realise until long afterwards that we were in the throes of the preliminaries to the Battle of Britain. What a time to marry!

Back at the shop we lived in the flat. My first housekeeping was to prepare the evening meal and whip it all into the shelter on a tray if we

Margo Hitchinson and Maurice Headford on their wedding day, August 1940.

were unable to eat it before the sirens went off. The real blitzes soon
began and Maurice rigged up some sleeping accommodation in the shelter
so that even during that famous thirteen hour raid in the winter we were
able to get some sleep during the lulls. On one occasion he chased a rat
around the shelter with his slipper before we settled down!

Soon things became really bad and often the gas supply would be cut
off for a few hours. As our shop oven was powered by gas it was a
catastrophe but we carried on as best we could. Our customers were now
friends and there was a wonderful spirit of camaraderie. When it was
possible we cooked bread and cakes which sold very quickly. We often
had to boil a kettle on the fire during gas and electricity cuts in the air

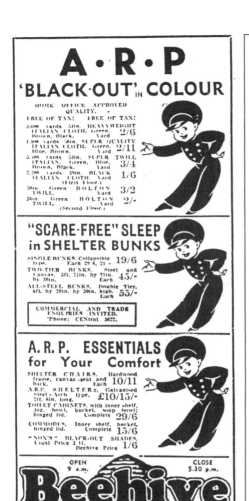

Whatever your share in the National task, BREAD — the supreme source of vigour and activity — will help you tackle the job with unflagging energy. Now, more than ever, your diet *must* include sufficient Bread. Eat it at every meal.

1940 advertisement in Birmingham Gazette. (Birmingham Museums & Art Gallery).

Britain needed bread for the war effort.

raids. The war demanded a strength and resourcefulness that seemed impossible at times.

One awful time vital water mains were badly damaged and we had no water for forty-eight hours. An old cottage not far away had a well in the garden and supplied everyone with water. A long patient queue formed outside the cottage gate all day, everyone carrying a bucket or some other receptacle. How we blessed the cottage and its kind occupants!

Scarcity of sugar led to sugar-less recipes.

Food such as sugar, tea and fats were very scarce by 1941 and rationing made life very difficult. When planning a meal, ration coupons had to be calculated as well as the cost. Tedious queues at shops became a fact of life. Papers and magazines were full of ideas for 'austerity cooking' with suggestions for fatless pastry, sugarless puddings, eggless cakes, meatless meals and fuelless cookery. The Ministry of Food recommended the ingenious hay-box where a porridge or stew could be transferred from the stove to a wooden box stuffed with hay or paper. There it would cook slowly throughout the day or night in conserved heat. Pigs Feet in Jelly, Calves Feet Pie, and Sheep's Head Broth were advocated for a change!

Cakes could be made to rise with the addition of household soda, potatoes were a substitute for flour and saccharine was used instead of sugar. Icing sugar was made illegal and there was a ban on all candied peels, crystallised cherries and sugar ornaments which made running a cake shop very difficult. Some brides even had to forego having an iced wedding cake and made do with cardboard covered cakes!

Ironically, the desire for sweet cakes was made worse by the stress of wartime conditions — nothing was so welcome as a homely cake in the shelter during an air raid! Typical wartime recipes recommended in magazines were Eggless Trench Cake, Baking Powder Rolls and Eggless Christmas Cake. It was a wonder that anybody even tried to cook puddings or cakes!

White bread also became a rarity when cheap supplies of grain from America were cut off. People were even fined for throwing bread to the birds. Despite the Ministry of Food extolling the virtues of dried egg powder no-one liked its rubbery, leathery taste but it was better than nothing. It became a popular hobby to keep hens, ducks and geese for the eggs and much bartering took place for items in short supply.

We wondered whether we would have to do some work for the war effort and had to appear before a tribunal. Attending this interview in fear and trembling we were asked what exactly we made. We answered them

Wartime advertisement in Birmingham Gazette. (Birmingham Museums & Art Gallery).

truthfully, the crucial question being "Do you make bread as well as cakes?". The answer was "Yes!", of course, but we did not inform them exactly how many loaves were made as they omitted to ask! We were delighted when we were told that it was in order for us to carry on our business as bread was an essential food. Twelve loaves a day had saved us!

We knew that currants, sultanas or raisins would be in short supply as the war progressed so we decided to secrete one box of fruit at the back of the pantry for the next Christmas. Twelve months later, during a time of severe shortages, we brought it out triumphantly, eager to make some Christmas cakes. The box was, as usual, made of wood and as we wrenched the top pieces off our smiles turned to looks of horror as that precious store of fruit was literally alive, a wriggling mass of white fat juicy grubs! Perhaps the box had been old stock in the first place but it had definitely been too long in our pantry. We also remembered, too late, that we had just had a very hot summer . . .

It was not a case of going out to buy another box. Fruit was practically

unobtainable at the time as the convoys were being decimated. We could
not afford to be squeamish or fastidious. We had to set to and pick out,
one by one, all those fat wriggly little bodies . . . ! I wished we knew a
fisherman but they were all away fighting a war. After we had carefully
washed and dried the fruit it all looked very normal and very innocent.
The finished Christmas cakes sold quickly and were much appreciated.
Needless to say we breathed no word to any customer but it was the stuff
of nightmares . . . !

We sometimes had daylight raids as well as at night and wondered if
we ought to dive under our heavy old-fashioned kitchen table. The Rover
factory was not far away and planes probably made this their target.
After 1942-3 raids abated and we settled down to some sort of routine.
Everything we made sold very quickly so we decided to shut the shop on
three afternoons a week. Our bank balances grew so we invested in
National Savings as we could find little to buy in the shops, except Utility
clothing and furniture. We were continually urged by the government to
'make do and mend'.

The Dig for Victory campaign became famous in 1942 – 3 when
vegetables were scarce and we were bombarded with nutritional
propaganda. Allotments flourished everywhere in the patriotic call to 'Dig
harder to beat the U-boat'. Potato Pete and Dr Carrot became familiar
cartoons and we were encouraged to :-

"Dig! Dig! Dig! And your muscles will grow big
Keep pushing in the spade!
Never mind the worms
Just ignore the squirms
And when your back aches laugh with glee!
And keep on diggin'
Till we give our foes a wiggin'
Dig! Dig! Dig to Victory!"

My husband Maurice took all this to heart and rented an allotment. For
many years he was known to allotment holders as "4 o'Clock", as no
one knew him by name! Cultivating his allotment proved to be an
occupational hobby which was to last him all his life, providing fruit and
vegetables for family and friends.

In the middle of 1943 I was delighted to find I was pregnant as I was
thirty years old. The flat was not very suitable for a baby so we looked
around for a house. We found one on Fox Hollies Road in Acocks Green
which was available for rent. The elderly owner had left it to go to her
relatives during the air raids. She refused to sell but we were convinced
she would never return. What pleased us most was the 'old world'
garden. Maurice was a gardener and the sunken lawn and surrounding
rockeries delighted us both.

I began looking for a pram but they were in short supply as almost overnight factories had changed to making munitions or aeroplanes. Women were lucky to find anything other than a Utility version which was just a box on wheels and very cumbersome. On a visit to Scarborough I found some prams far superior to the ones in Birmingham shops. I paid 10/- for a cream coloured one, having it sent by rail. My friend Joan was so impressed with it that she ordered one for her own baby.

In September 1943 I left the business, employing an accountant to discuss a termination settlement. Ethel moved into the flat and decided to carry on with the shop, helped by a widow who had been working for us for a while. The business continued until the early Fifties, although it was never quite the same.

My first daughter, Frances, was born in a great hurry during the blackout and a foggy night in November 1943. A few years later Barbara arrived. I was not sorry to leave the business at the time as maternity and domesticity seemed very attractive. I was very tired of living on the premises where there was always some job to be done. Only long afterwards did I realise that building up a business from scratch can probably only be done once in a lifetime. The first £1000 is said to be the hardest to make, which we had done. The agent must have been pleased that in spite of his tremendous doubts we were the first tenants to succeed in keeping the premises occupied as a viable business.

The property is still a cafe and seems to be a thriving business, now specialising in "he-men's breakfasts" and mixed grills for quite a different clientele. I hope the present tenants of our old shop are having half the fun we had in the good old days of "4 o'Clock"!

Advertisement in Vogue, 1940

CHAPTER 9

SPRING FARM

Spring Farm lies tucked away in the village of Thorpe Bassett on the edge of the Yorkshire Wolds which are smooth rounded hills with views stretching for miles. There are rolling cornfields and sheep pastures fringed with hedges and woodland. Neighbouring villages have intriguing names such as Scagglethorpe, Duggleby, Wetwang and Foxholes where the Southwell family have intermingled and intermarried with other farming families over the centuries.

The farm was built three hundred years ago and was enlarged by a gentleman farmer in the last century. At Spring Farm Margo Headford and her family enjoyed many happy holidays and the hospitality of her uncle, Richard (Dick) Southwell and his wife Jessie. As a tenant farmer Dick Southwell farmed Spring Farm with his son Tim, whose family shared the farm. Margo has many memories of life at the farm:-

In the large old-fashioned kitchen many a sickly lamb was brought in to be cosseted and given a bottle of milk on a bitterly cold winter's night. The lambs were always called "George" so that when the name was called to his flock in the field several lambs would rush up, hoping for an special treat.

The main crops grown were barley and wheat, with turnips and swedes for the sheep to feed on in the winter. Free-ranging hens were also kept and the children delighted in collecting eggs from the surrounding barns. I remember my uncle washing the eggs before they went to market as he got more money for clean ones. Young pheasants could also be seen

everywhere on the farm as the owners of the land employed a professional gamekeeper.

After harvest, the barns were full to bursting point with grain and every door used to have a little square cut out of it for the farm cats. All the cats had to earn their keep by catching rats and mice.

Spring Farm

Aunt Jessie used to feed the cats once a day with a conglomeration of bread, bacon rinds, meat and cat food. Opening the back door she would cry loudly, "Puss! Puss!". It was an amazing sight to see them come running from all directions — across the stackyard, along walls and over the barn roofs. Sometimes there were as many as twenty cats but all were quite wild except for one favoured superior cat who was allowed inside at times.

The spring that gives the farm its name has never been known to dry up so there must be a vast supply of water under the chalkland. This necessity of life runs from the stream into a pipe and then into a man-made reservoir, ready to be pumped up to a cistern in the roof for use in the farmhouse.

My uncle was once delighted to entertain and educate a party of local schoolchildren who were investigating for a project the source of their

local beck. After their visit to the farm they all penned letters to thank
him, one writing: "Thank you very much for showing us your sauces —
we enjoyed them very much"! If they had but known, he had enjoyed
their visit even more then they had, as he always enjoyed having an
audience!

After a tenancy of over fifty years at Spring Farm Jessie Southwell's funeral
was a splendid and honoured departure from this world, with the tiny village
church full and overflowing. For Dick Southwell, the burden of loneliness was
not easy to bear after a fifty-three year old partnership. His death a few years
later signified the end of an era, especially as it came only a fortnight after the
funeral of his sister, Madge, who had been almost a mother to Margo over the
years.

All the family have much enjoyed visiting that special peaceful corner of the
Yorkshire Wolds wherein lie some of our ancestral roots, so far from the noise
and bustle of the great industrial city of Birmingham.

A typical gentleman's outfit advertised in
Acocks Green and Solihull Journal, 1900

CHAPTER 10

AROUND FOX HOLLIES IN ACOCKS GREEN

After the war Margo Headford settled happily into domesticity, to raise a family and to enjoy a life of stability and security for the first time in many years. But neighbours on Fox Hollies Road were horrified when she admitted to eating mushrooms that her husband had picked from the grass verges on his way home from work, as she relates:-

We lived opposite Grey Gables and near the Warwick Road junction, behind some tall elm trees. In my childhood no doubt horses munched where our house was built. As a result we were able frequently to pick mushrooms along the edge of the pavement, especially when the weather was moist and warm. They were unmistakably mushrooms as we lived to tell the tale!

When I was young I used to walk from Sparkhill as far as the railway bridge on Shaftmoor Lane. I always thought I was in the country as there were few houses and a great many fields and trees. Even in the Thirties Fox Hollies Road was still a quiet narrow lane with many trees.

Fox Hollies Hall was standing then and a friend once told me that the grounds were always a challenge to him and all the other 'likely lads' of Acocks Green! The owner of the Hall, a certain Colonel Zaccheus Walker, known as 'old Zacchy', guarded his property well. Only the entrance posts to the old drive now remain as sentinels of another era and one of these has nearly perished. I wonder if the Colonel's ghost approves of the towering flats on what was once his pride and joy? They are named after fields on the estate — Holly Piece, Home Meadow, Coppice and Curtis Gardens.

Fox Hollies Hall was formerly a typical English country inn where hounds met and village sports and fetes were held. The name Fox Hollies probably comes from the Fox family who lived in the area from the fifteenth century, purchasing a farm from the Hollies family which became known as Foxholleys. The Hall was purchased by an earlier Mr Zaccheus Walker for his retirement. It was rebuilt in 1860 in an Italianate style with stables, kennel lodge, farm buildings and a gallery for the collection of paintings which was

Fox Hollies Road outside Fox Hollies Hall in the Twenties. (J. Marks)

frequently opened to the public. It became one of the most imposing houses in the district.

The first Zaccheus Walker, great grandfather to Colonel Walker of living memory, was born in 1736. He came to Birmingham to work with the famous Matthew Boulton of Soho and married his employer's sister, becoming a partner in a merchant's business, called 'Boulton and Walker' in Livery Street in Birmingham. His eldest son, Zaccheus II, also became a partner, travelling to Paris on business where he nearly lost his life in the Revolution.

Zaccheus Walker III was brought up by his uncle, Joseph Walker, when his father died at an early age. Zaccheus III inherited everything from his uncle, including the business 'Armitage and Walker' which he sold to retire to "the sylvan seclusion of Fox Hollies Hall", states *Yardley Newsletter* in 1896. Under the impression that Acocks Green would develop into an important residential suburb he made extensive purchases of land and enlarged the Hall in 1860. He died in 1890 and was buried in the family vault at Handsworth parish church.

Zaccheus Walker IV, the Colonel of living memory, was born at Handsworth in 1848 and went to Glasgow university where he qualified in Engineering Sciences. After working for a marine engineering firm he moved to London where he designed torpedo boats. When his father's health began to fail he settled at Fox Hollies Hall at the age of 32, enjoying agricultural pursuits of all kinds. He was successful in the breeding of shire-horses and hunters and was often seen judging at horse shows. He was a member of the Birmingham Hunt Committee and the North Warwickshire Hunt, and also bred a fine strain of bullmastiffs, being an expert in this field. In 1909 his dogs gained twenty seven first prizes at one show, according to an obituary on Joseph Smith who was his faithful kennel master for over fifty years.

Colonel Walker took an active interest in local affairs, supporting three cricket clubs and two football clubs. He somehow found time to be Vice-Chairman of the Yardley District Council, governor of Yardley Charity Estates, a member of the Solihull Board of Guardians, Chairman of Yardley Sanitary Authority and Yardley School Board and a Justice of the Peace in Worcestershire. He was also a patriotic Volunteer Officer in the reserve forces for over twenty years, having always yearned for a soldier's life, despite being a businessman. Presumably this is the origin of his title of Colonel, as he had a long and distinguished record in the Volunteer Engineer Corps and the Warwickshire and Worcestershire Volunteer Artillery.

Fox Hollies Hall c.1930. (Acocks Green Local History Society)

He was remarkably generous in allowing many people to enjoy the Hall and its beautiful grounds, including seven hundred poor children from All Saint's Ward in Birmingham on a Fresh Air Fund outing in 1896. A train conveyed the party to Acocks Green station, being met by Mr Walker on a fine black horse who led the procession and band along the roads to the Hall. Lunch was provided in a big marquee, after which there were games with many prizes. All the children also received buns and cakes for tea, followed by flowers, sweets and a toy to take home. Undoubtedly it was an outing to remember as so many of them had probably never had a day in the countryside.

In the same year a fete for St Mary's church extension fund was held at the Hall. The gardens and greenhouses were open to the public, a military band played and a concert was performed in the picture gallery. As reported by *Yardley Newsletter*, there were prizes for the best decorated pony carriages, bicycle races, "washing competitions and hat trimming competitions for the gentlemen"!

As a person Colonel Walker was very decisive, with a good sense of humour, according to *Yardley Newsletter*. He sold off his estate to the City of Birmingham after the First World War as land was needed for development, on the condition he had the right to live there for as long as he liked. After his death in 1930 the Hall was demolished and the flats were erected.

Many people still remember from the Twenties how dark the lane seemed outside the Hall which lay back in the trees behind big hedges, railings and two beautiful gates. There were often large dogs roaming about the grounds, causing fear and trepidation to passers-by. There was very little traffic on Fox Hollies Road, apart from the occasional horse and cab. It began to be developed in the Thirties when houses and shops near Olton Boulevard were built. The tree-clad central reservation on the major part of Fox Hollies Road was intended to be a tram track but it never materialised. Living up to its name, foxes were often to be seen in the vicinity.

Olton Boulevard and Greenwood Avenue were constructed in the Thirties as spacious roads with beautiful trees planted all along. Mrs Edmonds, an elderly resident of Grey Gables, remembers the coachloads of people who used to travel to see Greenwood Avenue where she lived. It seemed as if the municipal planners were proud of it. Her daughter, Connie Hawkes, recalls that the builder's workmen borrowed their English Toy Fox Terrier to catch all the rats in the area when Greenwood Avenue was built and over five hundred trees were planted. Greenwood Avenue finished at Hartfield Crescent in those days and was bordered by fields of horses and cows. A foal was killed in a thunderbolt in a storm in 1931. Shirley Road was just a lane bordered with hedges and high banks and the whole area was very rural with fields and farms.

Margo and Maurice Headford lived opposite Grey Gables Retirement Home which was opened by and named after the city's Lord Mayor, Sam Grey, who lived in Acocks Green. It was a home for "retired gentlewomen in reduced circumstances" and had previously been called "Mayfield". As a private house it had been there since the turn of the century, standing isolated on that side of Fox Hollies Road between the Warwick Road and Mayfield Road. In the Thirties the house was occupied by a family who manufactured lime-spraying equipment. When they moved, the house remained empty until it was opened as a Home.

There was a small triangular plot of land on Fox Hollies Road, behind the houses which were opposite Grey Gables. The land was bordered by other houses on the Warwick Road and Westfield Road. It had been allotments in the First World War and became a wilderness for children to play in, as Dorothea Abbott recalls:-

It was full of blackberry bushes, old raspberry canes and all sorts of long grass which was just right for playing hide-and seek and making dens. In fact, it was a paradise for us children in the Twenties! We had "den feasts" in the middle of rose-bay willowherbs, with picnics of food begged from our parents. I remember we even had a concert, with children dancing and singing "Teddy Bears Picnic"! We very much resented those housewives who came there to pick raspberries and we used to crawl about in the undergrowth pretending they were our enemies! During World War II it became an allotment again and my father and Maurice Headford had a plot there.

This area where we played used to belong to Dr Cordley Bradford who owned a large Victorian building, constructed in red brick with tall chimneys, called "Merstowe". It was on the corner of Broad Road (originally called Broad Lane), and the Warwick Road. In the Thirties the house was demolished and was built over by a road of new houses — called Merstowe Close.

I remember Dr Bradford as a nice old man who kept two horses and a big mastiff dog. He also owned the field opposite his house, on the Warwick Road, where he sometimes kept his horses. Adjoining the field on the corner of Flint Green Road were some very picturesque half timbered Tudor cottages inhabited by Dr Bradford's groom and gardener, Mr Wilcox. The cottages are still remembered by many local people and were sadly demolished in the Thirties.

Dr Bradford would often come to talk to us as we gathered round a big oak tree which was by the hedge bounding his field and taught us how to give sugar to a horse. He was tall and had a dark beard — a thoroughly Victorian character. His daughter married Dr Leigh Hadley who had a house nearby on the Warwick Road, but died in childbirth.

Dr Bradford had lived in Acocks Green since about 1880 and was a familiar figure in the area for his medical services and for his gig. He also

The old cottage on Flint Green Road, taken by G. Lewis, the local photographer c.1904. (J. Marks)

did a lot of public work, being a churchwarden at St Mary's church and President of Acocks Green Institute.

On the corner of Fox Hollies Road and Warwick Road was a very dirty Victorian factory. Between 7 a.m. and 8 a.m. we heard many footsteps of people walking to work there, going past our house on the Warwick Road. I remember that a great hooter used to sound at 7.55 a.m. precisely!

This factory was called the Pioneer Cabinet Works, earlier known as the Birmingham Woven Wire Mattress Company Limited. It closed down in 1933 and was demolished a year or two later. It was originally run by Messrs. Waterhouse and Blantern and was "rather a dreary, drab looking building with its dark blue brick walls and iron barred windows more resembling a prison than a place of work", according to Mr J. V. Tustin in *Acocks Green's District Advertiser*.

Thomas Walley Blantern was, in fact, a local councillor who lived in Flint Green Road and was a well-known member of Acocks Green Liberal Club. He patented six inventions for the firm which were very successful. Every detail of the process of making wire mattresses was done on the premises, according to 1895 *Yardley Newsletter*. Huge logs of timber were sawn up and there were workshops for planing, drilling, boring and polishing. The factory later made furniture.

Pioneer cabinet works catalogue shows a double bed with Jacobean mouldings (£25) and a single bed with twist turnings (£9.15.0), 1920.

1950 advertisements.

Further up Fox Hollies Road was once a very pleasant country walk, called Nine Stiles Walk. It started on the Stratford Road, near York Road in Hall Green, going by the dirt track stadium for dog racing. The walk continued across Fox Hollies Road, through Nine Stiles to the Shirley Road and beyond to the Gospel Oak.

Alongside the walk, just off Fox Hollies Road, Nine Stiles allotments were opened in 1953. A pavilion and other amenities were provided for allotment holders and it was a thriving concern for many years. Maurice Headford rented a plot when the allotment behind their house closed down. He became the treasurer of Nine Stiles Allotments for many years and in his retirement especially enjoyed the company of fellow gardeners and a chat in the pavilion. All his family and friends enjoyed the fruits of his labours until ill health in old age forced him to give it up. Gardening had provided him with a life-long hobby and a long association with Fox Hollies Road.

Margo and Maurice Headford lived in Fox Hollies Road for forty six years and Number 52 was the focus of many a family gathering until illness caused them both to leave their home. Maurice continued to take a great interest in the health and welfare of his daughters' beans and other vegetables growing in their gardens. The wartime 'Dig for Victory' campaign had certainly made its mark!

CHAPTER 11

ALONG THE YARDLEY ROAD IN ACOCKS GREEN

The arrival of the Great Western railway station in 1852 opened up the Yardley Road for wealthy businessmen and residents from the centre of Birmingham. It became possible to commute into the city for work from a clean and pleasant country district. The parish of Yardley in Worcestershire was a place of farms, narrow country lanes and picturesque cottages.

The Yardley Road developed as a secondary shopping and residential area in the hamlet of Acocks Green, previously known as Westley Brook. In the 1880's there were only five houses on the Yardley Road, according to an account in *Acocks Green, Olton and Solihull Journal* in 1912. It was a country lane with irregular grass-bordered footpaths and high hedges on either side.

Large villas were soon built on the Sherbourne Road south of the station for the homes of wealthy people from Birmingham. Very few of the houses had coach accommodation as the railway was used for transport. Large terraced villas were built on Flint Green Road and by 1903 three streets of endless terraced houses sprang up north of the station — Alexander Road, Douglas Road and Florence Road. The Avenue, Malvern Road and Elmdon Road were already built. Some of the older and larger residences included Cottesbrook House (on the site of Cottesbrook Road) and the Beeches (on the site of Beeches Avenue) which was a mansion in rustic Tudor style. By 1911 the Yardley Road near the Swan at South Yardley had many villas and terraces amongst the cottages. The station had to be re-built to cope with the growing number of people using the line. In those days there were coal fires in the station waiting rooms and roses on the platforms.

In 1926 the Outer Circle bus route ended the isolation of Yardley village and the Yardley Road. Industry developed at Hay Mills and Tyseley, including Charles Churchill Machine Tools, Wilmot Breedon and Rover cars. At the same time farms still existed in the area on Stockfield Road and Waterloo Road.

The Great Western Hotel had been built alongside the station and became a social centre for the area, noted for the country dancing in its garden. The station reached its heyday when Wyman's bookstall on the platform had a manager and four boys. The manager was Alfred Wells who had first worked for Wyman's on Snow Hill station and later started his own newsagent's shop in Acocks Green in 1914. He was a keen photographer, taking numerous

Great Western Hotel & Railway Station, Acocks Green, c.1908. The station was enlarged in 1906, with the population of Acocks Green rising from 3,836 in 1901 to 8,605 in 1911. (J. Marks)

postcard views of Acocks Green. His business in Acocks Green became one of the best known shops in the village, selling toys as well as papers and magazines.

A small hamlet called Tenchlee or Tenchley once existed on the Yardley Road where Wynford Road and Mansfield Road join the main road near the Warwick and Birmingham Canal bridge. On the canal at Yardley Wharf T. Boston and Sons once had their long-standing coal business, supplying coal, anthracite and coalite which was brought by canal from the Black Country. The Warwick and Birmingham Canal had been a tremendous feat of engineering, being built in six years between 1793 – 1799 by huge gangs of navvies. Much traffic must have left the busy Warwick Road at that time, relieving coachmen of driving a team of six to eight horses on heavy lumbering wagons.

George Muscott and Sons also had their well-known tannery business on the Yardley Wharf for many years — many people still remember the smell that came from it! George Muscott, a local councillor, started Acocks Green's first fire brigade in 1895 with six officers, 500 foot of hose and a manual machine.

A well-known business further along the Yardley Road, not strictly in Acocks Green but in South Yardley, is William H. Painter Limited, the undertakers. Starting in 1907 on the corner of Church Road, the business moved to its present site on the Yardley Road corner in 1938. Originally

1911 advertisements.

the premises stabled twenty Belgian black horses and had a staff of twelve coachmen. It was self-contained with a harness room and a smithy. Horses were broken in there and on frosty mornings special cogs were put in their hooves to stop them slipping. Each driver had to clean their own harness and polish the black leather.

1934 advertisement.

1900 (left), 1925 (right) advertisements.

The horses took part in many local shows and carriages were hired out for special occasions such as weddings. Hansom cabs and landaus were also available for hire until the motor car took over in 1938. In the old days a team of black horses leading a glass-sided hearse was the dignified and acceptable way of departing this world in an elegant manner. The wonderful collection of old photographs at the firm gives an insight into a bygone age.

The striking police station on the Yardley Road was built in 1909 in the days of Worcestershire County. It accommodated two sergeants, one married constable, fourteen single constables and cost £789, replacing an earlier station on the Warwick Road on the site of Acocks Green school. Nearby was the fire station on Alexander Road, opposite the Baptist Church which had been designed in 1903 by the architect Francis Andrews.

Between Douglas Road and Harold's Garage (previously Roberts' Garage) was a row of shops depicted on several postcards in the Twenties and Thirties. The shops included John Coleman, The Birmingham Co-operative Limited, George Mason the grocer, Wheeler's cooked meats, William Parker the draper, Walter Biddle the draper and William Dunn the confectioner.

The coffin van which was used by William Painter the Undertakers until the Thirties. (W. H. Painter Ltd)

Another row of shops was situated between Cottesbrook Road and the canal on the Yardley Road. In 1925 they included Morris's circulating library of four thousand books. Next door was Gilbert's shoe shop which advertised it was a "smart boot store, selling bargains from 6/9."

Not far from the Baptist Church in the Thirties and Forties was "4 o'Clock" cafe and cake shop, at Number 73 Yardley Road, being one of a row of four shops built opposite Cottesbrook Road in 1935. The other three shops were a hairdresser at Number 75 (changing hands from Mrs Meek to Mrs Greves); Thomas Todd the wine merchant at Number 77; and a ladies fashion shop at Number 77 which rapidly changed hands several times.

A neighbouring business was 'Harold's Garage', owned by Harold Cheshire who recalls:-

On the other side of "4 o'Clock", across an passage, was a small isolated stationary shop run by Miss Gertrude Sutton at Number 69. It was also a lending library, and was owned by Mr Myatt of Harborne who was a member of the Myatt Razor Blade family, well-known in the Twenties and Thirties.

The passage between "4 o'Clock" and Miss Sutton's shop led to a very large house, called "The Beeches", which was demolished about 1935 and replaced with four shops including 4 o'Clock and Beeches Avenue. The Beeches was tenanted by a very old man who had a very old car and he was looked after by a very old woman — altogether very dark and spooky!

Further down the road were three more large residences, one of which belonged to the Neale family who were well-known silver-smiths in the Birmingham Jewellery Quarter. My wife, Lily, had her first situation there, looking after Miss Neale.

Opposite the garage were two large residences, one of which was tenanted by Mr Hoskins of Hoskins and Sewell, the famous Bedstead and Ship's Berths manufacturers. In the Thirties these houses were demolished and a row of five shops were built on the site. Another three shops were added at the left-hand side of the row, up to Cottesbrook Road where a school was built in 1933. Norris and Jarvis, the well-known iron mongers, were in this row of shops for many years.

Robert's 1925 advertisement.

I started my business in 1929 and it lasted many years until 1965. I began work at Colman Roberts' Garage as an apprentice mechanic in 1925, when I was eighteen years old. Mr Roberts joined Mr Colman in the early Twenties, renting the shop and workshop. He also collected the rents of twenty lock-up garages which were situated behind the garage. Mr Roberts was the motor engineer while Mr Colman attended to the books and the shop. Mr Colman also ran a lawn-mowing business, using a B.S.A. motor-cycle box side-car for transport, one of his customers being the Malvern Tennis Club.

Yardley Road, looking towards Acocks Green, from Roberts Garage. The car being repaired by Mr J. Roberts was a 1922 Wolseley. c.1926.
(H. Cheshire)

When Mr Colman and Mr Roberts had some lock-up garages built beside Acocks Green station I took over Colman and Roberts' business in 1929. I was unable to pay the necessary £250 for stock, workshop and one petrol pump so borrowed some money from Mr A. Lincoln and Mr Bernard Pitt who ran a nearby chemist's shop and kindly put in £80 each to help me get started. I also borrowed £50 from my father. The stock consisted of a small number of B.S.A. cycles, a few second-hand motor-cycles, two oil cabinets and a storage bin for cans of petrol.

There was a pit in the workshop and many were the hours I spent down there until the early hours of a morning. I worked on the basis of 2/6 an hour, including overheads, for car repairs — and 1/6 an hour, or less, for cycle repairs. Times were very hard! I had to open six and a half days a week for many years. I must say that I had many good friends who enjoyed "mucking in" to help and later on I had help in the shop from my wife Lily and my daughter Ann. For a miserly commission I collected the garage rents which was often a difficult task and also sold bicycles, mo-peds, spares and accessories for motor-vehicles.

I can remember walking in to "4 o'Clock" one day and being

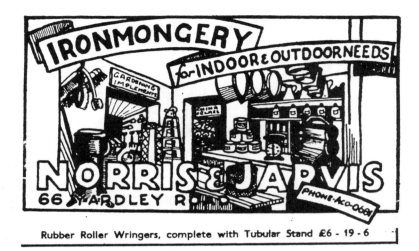

Norris & Jarvis 1940's advertisement.

J. HUTCHINS & SON
*(Late Foreman for
T. Price & Son, Acocks Green.)*

Painters, Plumbers, Decorators.

ESTIMATES FREE.

192, Yardley Road, ACOCKS GREEN,
BIRMINGHAM.

R. Jeffery
Watchmaker & Jeweller
For Silver Plate and Fancy Jewellery
43 Yardley Road,   Acocks Green
Tel.: ACO 2018

Shop advertisements 1925 – 1932.

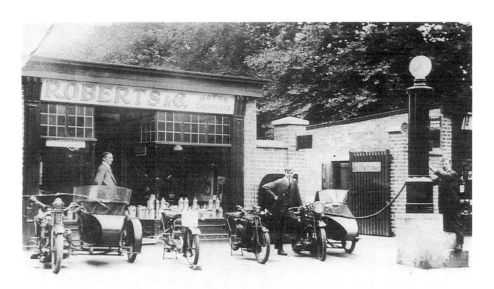

Roberts Garage in 1926, showing partners Mr J. Roberts and Mr F. Colman, and Mr H. Cheshire as an apprentice mechanic. (H. Cheshire)

Harold's Garage in 1936, with Harold Cheshire, the proprietor, in front of the shop. (H. Cheshire)

confronted by two attractive young ladies sitting on the counter and dangling their pretty legs! They informed me they were setting up a cafe and made a tempting array of cakes, large and small, plain and fancy. They also cooked some lunches at one time, particularly for the school teachers from the school which was opposite their shop. One of my clients, who came all the way from Erdington to have his car repaired, always went to their shop and bought chocolate biscuits which we consumed while he waited!

When we heard the radio announcement of war on the 3rd of September 1939 I remember I was working on a Mr Soden's car. We all expected air raids to come at any time. Gas masks and corrugated shelters were being supplied by the government and we expected to have to use them. Our shelter was not delivered until after the first air raids so we used to get under a heavy table. Although the sirens went on several occasions they were generally false alarms but we often heard the German aircraft overhead on their way to other targets. We heard them when Coventry was heavily bombed and could see the light of the fires in the sky.

There was a barrage balloon station close to the garage and about a hundred yards away was an anti-aircraft gun near the Yardley Road. When the raids started in earnest I joined the A.R.P. and the local fire-watching parties. Our local fire-watching squad had to operate in the back room of a butcher's shop so everything was very "meaty"! When it was a quiet night I spent quite a bit of time at Greenwood's Bakery in the room behind the shop. My favourite occupation was making holes in doughnuts and putting in the jam!

Birmingham, like Coventry, had one or two particularly bad nights. There was much house and factory destruction in Acocks Green and Tyseley. In fact, in nearby Cottesbrook Road two houses were destroyed but the occupants had a remarkable escape as they were in their shelters at the time. My wife's family, who lived in Spring Road in Tyseley, also had their house destroyed when they were in their shelter. My wife's sister had a large piece of shrapnel in her thigh and her father lost one eye, never really recovering from the shock.

Although our district was not amongst the most devastated areas, I sometimes wonder how we carried on with little sleep, day or night, for quite a long time. We had to make wide detours to get into the city of Birmingham as there were many bomb craters. When Birmingham had its heaviest air raids, two or three nights in succession, there was very little mains water at the hydrants to fight the fires. Had there been a further raid the next night we felt that Birmingham would have been finished as there was literally no water available! Many people left for the country in their cars before nightfall. You can imagine the relief when the sirens were silent!

1942 advertisement.

Many years have passed since the war yet strong memories remain of life in those difficult times when fortunes were made or lost. Life goes on following a pattern on the Yardley Road as "Harold's Garage" is now a second-hand car business and "4 o'Clock" is a workman's cafe. Perhaps we should take Sir Walter Scott's advice — to "look back, and smile at perils past".

The C.T.C. Gazette   ADVERTISEMENTS   DECEMBER, 1934

Quality counts in the LONG RUN

DON'T DECIDE TILL YOU'VE SEEN THE

RALEIGH
THE ALL-STEEL BICYCLE

From start to finish a Raleigh is planned by experienced and successful cyclists— men who have spent half their lives with their feet on pedals. So when they designed the Raleigh they did not have to **guess** what was wanted. They **knew.** That is why you find that all the little details fit in so well with your own ideas. The Raleigh is a machine for men who know what's what in a bicycle. It's good policy to wait till you've seen a Raleigh.

From £4-19-6 Cash or 10/- monthly (no deposit), fitted with Dunlop tyres, Brooks' saddle and the best of everything. Specify the Sturmey-Archer 3-speed gear, 20/- extra. Send post card for free copy of " The Book of the Raleigh " and name and address of nearest dealer.

**The RALEIGH CYCLE Co., Ltd.,
NOTTINGHAM.**
Depots and Agents Everywhere

Fit the Sturmey-Archer 3-speed gear—the gear that "makes cycling easy,

B.S.A. Tradesman's Bicycle

Trademan's bicycle - "a necessity for every business where prompt delivery of goods is essential". £16.

CHAPTER 12

ACOCKS GREEN IN THE DAYS OF HORSES

By 1836 the streets of central Birmingham echoed to the clatter of horses hooves and the metalled wheels of horse buses. Acocks Green had to wait quite a few more years for such a service.

Apart from the railway which had reached Acocks Green in 1852 there was no other means of travelling to Birmingham, except by stagecoach or personal horse-drawn carriage. Many local inhabitants in the village kept a gig. The regular link for parcels was by "old Willcox" the carrier who plied daily between the village and the city with his horse-van from Knowle.

The first horse omnibus travelled to Acocks Green about 1860 or 1870. It went down the Stratford Road from Birmingham to the Mermaid before branching out along the hazardous Warwick Road with all its humped bridges and bad surfaces. Abraham Whitehouse was the entrepreneur who extended his Stratford Road horse-bus service to Acocks Green on Sundays. A Mr Caswell also operated a Sunday service as far as Knowle from 1862. Tyseley Hill often proved to be a difficult obstacle for the horse-buses and a third horse was sometimes hitched on for extra power.

The turnpike abolition in 1872 helped to clear the way for better public transport. Before the Birmingham to Warwick Turnpike Act of 1725 was abolished, travellers from Acocks Green had to pass through various toll-gates on their journey to the city, including the Mermaid in Sparkhill and the Angel in Sparkbrook. There was also a toll-gate in Acocks Green between the old Dolphin Inn and Woodberry Walk, for which someone paid £365 in 1793 but only collected toll-money of £293 in his first year.

A weighbridge was installed at the Acocks Green toll-gate and tolls were reckoned according to the weight of the vehicle. In 1830 a toll for a four wheeled coach was 4d., a horse-wagon was 5d., a horse 1d. and sheep or pigs were 5d. per score. Tolls were exceedingly unpopular and the poor toll-keeper was often beaten up and his gates knocked down! Local farmers were exempt from the toll so they often operated a clandestine ferrying service.

Coaching inns provided an important function for travellers in the days when the average speed of a horse-drawn coach was only 10 miles per hour. Inns in Acocks Green provided horse troughs and fresh horses as well as food and rest for weary travellers. Most old inns kept horses for hire and were able to serve meals at any time. They were truly "public houses" where people

This two horse bus to Acocks Green needed a third horse for the hill at Tyseley. On the top deck 'garden' seats were provided for hardy passengers. (Millbrook House Ltd)

EARLY 19ᵗʰ CENTURY TOLL-GATE

1900 advertisement.

could go after business, to wait for transport or have a meal and a gossip with friends. In fact, they acted as headquarters for societies and clubs and often became the social centres of the district.

The Dolphin Inn was well-known just outside Acocks Green on the Warwick Road near the Olton boundary. This was the edge of the countryside when the Warwick Road was just a narrow and winding roadway. It was a picturesque old building, run for many years at the beginning of this century by Walter Padgett.

THE DOLPHIN INN, ACOCKS GREEN.

The old Dolphin Inn on the Warwick Road. This view was taken by George Lewis, the local photographer who had a business in the village, c.1905.

MAIL COACH

In 1785 John Palmer had started the Post Office mail coaches which ran daily. These coaches kept remarkably good times and it was unusual for one to be more than five minutes late on its run between London and Birmingham. In 1836 the mail coaches travelled a distance of 119 miles in 11 hours 56 minutes. This included all stops, with a dozen changes of horses, travelling via Banbury, Southam, Warwick and Solihull. The maximum length of time allowed for a change of horses on a mail coach was generally five minutes and it was sometimes done in one and a half!

The Royal Mail horse-van from Warwick to Birmingham used to call every night at Acocks Green post office. Local boys from Westley Brook cottages, opposite the post office, used to earn a few pence delivering telegrams and always used to view the arrival of the mail van with great excitement. Eventually the service was taken over by the railway and motor transport.

The advent of motor transport caused unemployment for many who were concerned with the welfare of horses, especially when many of the best horses disappeared to France for the First World War. Long distance coaches could not compete with the railways so they disappeared within a few years. By 1909 most horse drawn hackney cabs in the city had been replaced by motor cars.

However, horses were still used in the Twenties and Thirties for the daily deliveries of bread and milk, and most rag-and-bone men had a fleabitten horse and a goldfish bowl slung underneath the cart. People related strongly to individual horses who were always keen for a lump of sugar. Children loved following the horse vans on their rounds, watching the baker deliver his bread or the milkman ladle out the milk from a churn. One particular Midland Counties milkman in Acocks Green in the Twenties was Mr Jones, who was

Midland Counties children's painting competition in 1928 illustrates the horse-drawn milk float and a two pint bottle.

1911 advertisement, 1898 advertisement.

The old Smithy, run by Mr Harris, on the Warwick Road opposite Stockfield Road. A notice advertises 'Dancing, picnics, pierrots, airguns, cricket, bowls, tennis at Mount Cottage Farm, Shirley.' (H. Scott)

known as "Little Tich" because of his size. He had a winning smile for everyone.

Many farms surrounding Acocks Green used horses exclusively and existed for a long time alongside the increasing urban development, taking advantage of the saddlers and corn merchants in the district. The 1906 map shows clearly Fox Green Farm on the Westley Road, Stockfield Farm on Stockfield Road, Tyseley Farm on Knights Lane and Redstone Farm on the Warwick Road near the Olton boundary. Eventually they all disappeared, overcome by the polluted atmosphere where crops refused to ripen. There was also the problem of vandalism, trespass and trying to keep livestock within farm boundaries in an urban environment.

One of the busiest establishments in the district must have been the old smithy on the Warwick Road on the border of Tyseley, opposite the Congregational church on the Stockfield Road. Mr Harris was the blacksmith who shod horses from far and near, while his daughter kept a little shop in the adjoining cottage. At the turn of the century the Warwick Road by the smithy was very narrow and dusty. The forge was a busy place where grooms, carters and local tradesmen met and chatted while horses were shod by the blacksmith and his stalwart sons. Blacksmiths served many customers, including long distance waggonners, carriers, private carriage and cart owners as well as the local tradesmen.

Dorothea Abbott grew up in Acocks Green in the Twenties and recounts her memories of life in the days of horses:-

As a child of the Twenties I was lucky enough to live on the main Warwick Road at the Tyseley end of Acocks Green. When first we went to live there in 1925 it was still possible to take a country walk over the city boundary into Warwickshire or even one to green fields in Tyseley! Next door to the nearby Britannia Inn, opposite Stockfield Road, was the forge where grimy men in leather aprons shoed horses to the accompaniment of clanging anvils and the frightening heat from the fire.

There were few cars around in the early Twenties — in fact, our favourite game was to sit upstairs counting them! They were mostly black or khaki, with soft hoods and "dickies" at the back where two people could ride in the open.

The sound of horses hooves reverberated all through my childhood. I used to walk along mesmerised by the slow clip-clop of the large cart horses, which seemed always to be saying "Inkum-Clopla! Inkum-Clopla!".

One never to be forgotten Saturday afternoon my father took us along the Shirley Road to do the Nine Stiles walk. As we were wearily returning we were actually given a lift homewards by a kindly driver of a passing horse and cart. Lifted up to sit on the broad plank that served as a seat for the driver we felt like royalty as we jolted along!

Brewers' drays and station waggons were all drawn by sturdy horses.

Joseph Boston of T. Boston and Sons, coalmerchants of Acocks Green, c.1910. (John Whybrow Ltd)

DO YOU KNOW

" The cheapest place to get the best <u>COAL</u> from ? "

IT IS FROM **JOSEPH BOSTON,**

Your enquiries and orders will **YARDLEY WHARF,**
be esteemed. **.. ACOCKS GREEN.**

J. Boston advertisement, 1900.

Their brasses jingled and their noisy hooves struck sparks from the cobbled roads. May Day was especially exciting as we looked for the coloured ribbons the horses wore around their manes and tails. We were easily amused in those days!

The butchers all sent out boys in dainty light two wheeled gigs, to collect orders from their wealthier customers and to deliver the meat in time for lunch. These natty little outfits were driven along at a spanking pace by dashing young men in blue and white striped overalls making good use of the long light whips. The hooves of their speedy horses made quite a different sound on the road.

At a slower rate went the milk carts, stopping every few yards for the large two-pint bottles to be delivered on door steps. Their horses knew the rounds so well that they would often walk on to the next house if the milkman was inordinately long in making his doorstep transactions. One local farmer in Shaftsmoor Lane had a cart with two large rubber wheels and sold milk from a churn, using a dipper to fill the jugs brought to him by customers.

Bakers, laundries and coal merchants all used horses for deliveries and often the animals were given nose-bags of bran or oats to keep them happy while waiting for their drivers. The horses had a way of throwing back their heads and blowing into the bags to obtain the last remnants.

"Oi! Your 'orse can't get 'is gas-mask on!".
(Punch, 21 January 1941)

One of William Painter's elegant hearses which were used until the Thirties.
(W. H. Painter Ltd)

When passing by, one often came in for a shower of chaff and found oneself inhaling the horse's odorous breath, which as a child I found particularly distasteful!

Stone horse troughs were placed in strategic places, often outside public houses, to provide water for the thirsty beasts and were part of the street furniture, as were the mounting blocks of former days. Another part of the scene were the young entrepreneurs with shovels and little wooden carts who darted in and out of the traffic, picking up the horse droppings. Later they knocked on doors, hopefully asking, "Want any horse manure, missus?". The clatter of hooves, cries of "Whoa!" and "Gee-up!" all enlivened the streets, with the odd runaway horse adding a touch of drama.

Funeral carriages were always drawn by elegant black horses with long tails and manes. At their approach, most people would stand still until the cortege had passed, as a mark of respect. Mounted police, on their lovely dappled greys, are still with us.

There were both a saddler's and a corn chandler's in Acocks Green village, although at the time I had a very hazy idea of their function. I loved the saddler's with its leathery smell and pondered on the contents of the mysteriously bulging sacks in the dry dusty atmosphere of the corn chandler's shop.

I'm glad the last kick of the horse era did not pass without having some first class experience of those noble animals. As a land army girl I had to help once to harness a cart horse and to lead him up and down the field while a farm worker guided the hoe behind. I stumbled up and down the rows, trying to keep out of the way of those enormous legs.

What internal combustion engine has a sixth sense? Horses have been known to stop before a tree crashed down on a road and they have a sense or spirit which in man has atrophied. We lost something when horses passed out of everyday use, something rough but gentle — the relationship of a man with his beast — and we are the poorer for it. I feel privileged that my childhood was set well and truly in the days of horses.

Police horse cartoon. (Punch, 1932)

CHAPTER 13

ACOCKS GREEN FROM VILLAGE TO SUBURB

Acocks Green was just a small hamlet in the 1880's, with only eight shops in the village and one postman who also worked as the librarian, newsagent and grocer, according to some reminiscences in the 1912 *Acocks Green, Olton and Solihull Journal*. The village had been firmly placed in the County of Worcester since the Norman Conquest and was a peaceful country district in the parish and ancient Manor of Yardley until the year of 1911, when it became part of Greater Birmingham. It became a very select and desirable area on the outer edge of the big city.

Going further back into history, the Earls of Warwick held the Manor of Yardley for over two hundred years, until it reverted back to the crown estates of King Henry VII in 1487. In 1533 the Manor was granted to Catherine of Aragon in the year of her divorce from King Henry VIII. John Dudley, Duke of Northumberland, an ambitious man in political power who had been one of Henry VIII's most valued servants, was the next person to receive the Manor in 1553. He forfeited his estates to the crown later that year when he was executed for supporting the Lady Jane Grey, his daughter-in-law, in her claim to the throne after the death of the young King Edward VI. However, Queen Mary soon reinstated the Manor to the Dudley family, where it remained until it was sold in 1615 to Sir Roland Lacy. A few years later it was sold again to the Grevis family until John Taylor, a wealthy Birmingham manufacturer, purchased it in 1786. It remained in his family for many years until the manorial system gradually decayed.

Acocks Green Village, c.1900.

The name Acocks Green derives from the Acock family. The earliest recorded landowner, John Akok or Akoc, witnessed a Yardley deed in 1420. His family name became 'Acocke' in 1468 and 'Acock' in 1588 when William Acock purchased lands in the parish. In 1626 a William Acock, son of Richard Acock of Acocks Green, was given as a marriage settlement "Acocks Green House and other estates". The house can be seen on maps as recent as 1938, situated between the Great Western Railway line and the main Warwick Road, opposite the old Dolphin Inn. It was demolished to make way for a block of flats in Woodcock Lane. The Acock family appear to have left the district after Richard Acock had been buried in 1774 in Yardley church.

G.W.R. Locomotive. 1845.

In 1845 a great feat of engineering took place in Acocks Green with the construction of the Great Western Railway which was designed by the famous engineer, Isambard Kingdom Brunel. The digging of railway cuttings was all done by hand by huge gangs of "navigators", or "navvies" as they were called. Some embankments were quite enormous, such as the section of the line through Acocks Green and Olton which needed a cutting one mile long and thirty feet deep, with an embankment up to forty feet in height. The men took great pride in their arduous work, being tough, honest and good hearted as well as being so well paid they could easily afford plenty of good food and other luxuries.

Acocks Green and South Yardley Station opened on October 1st 1852, being at the time the first station on the line from Birmingham. It consisted of one or two wooden sheds on a platform, a porter, a lad and two signalmen who had to walk fifty yards up the line to pull the signals by hand. The first stationmaster to be appointed in 1857 was Mr J. Harmer. He remained in his post for over twenty years, being superseded in 1879 by Mr Richard Groves.

The station opened up the area for wealthy businessmen who came out of the smoke to settle in the hamlet and to commute to work in the city. It also became a very select place to live for people in retirement. There was a rapid expansion in the second half of the nineteenth century, with four main areas developing:- Yardley Road, the hamlet of Flint Green on the Warwick Road,

Acocks Green Station opened in 1852 as part of the Great Western Railway. This photograph taken by George Lewis shows the station before it was enlarged in 1906. (M. Clarke)

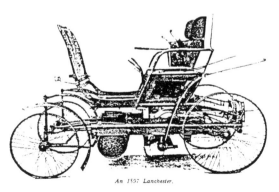

An 1897 Lanchester.

The Lanchester was one of the first cars to be owned by a local resident.

Westley Brook hamlet which became Acocks Green village and the area around the Dolphin Inn on the Warwick Road near Olton which had several cottages and farms.

Many large houses were built near Acocks Green village on the Warwick Road opposite St Mary's church, most of them having coach houses and stables for carriages or two-wheeled dog carts. Some coach houses had a room above for the coachman who often served as the gardener or manservant in the household.

In one of the houses known as Stone Hall lived Joseph Bourne, a gun manufacturer. Stone Hall became the Adult Education Centre while another big house is now Churchill Citizens Club. Neighbouring houses were once occupied by Dr Bostock Hill, the Medical Officer for the City of Birmingham, and the Playfairs family who were Birmingham businessmen. One house was requisitioned in the First World War to house Belgian refugees.

At The Corinthians, another large house on the Warwick Road, lived Mr Joseph Taylor who is famous for being the first person in the village to own a motor-car. He caused much terror to local horse-drawn traffic with his 1898 Lanchester and its tiller steering! His chauffeur used to wear a black leather outfit with leggings and goggles, much to the amusement of local children.

Congregational Church and School on Stockfield Road, showing the new 1895 extensions. (Yardley Newsletter)

Another resident on the Warwick Road was Arthur Gaskin who was the Head of the Birmingham School of Jewellery with the Birmingham College of Art. The family were all artistic, being members of the Birmingham School of Artists about 1880 – 90. In fact, the whole area was much sought after by the wealthy families of Birmingham until the Thirties when they all began to move further out to Solihull, Knowle and Dorridge. At one time in the Twenties Acocks Green was called "Snobs Green" when many families began moving in from Sparkhill and Small Heath!

Further up the Warwick Road a hamlet developed near Fox Hollies Road which included the Congregational church, the Smithy, an old house called the

Acocks Green Methodist Church. (J. R. Taylor)

Grange and the first industry of the area, the Birmingham Wire Mattress Company.

The Congregational church on the corner of Stockfield Road was built in 1860, before the foundation St Mary's church in Acocks Green village. For many years it was known as the 'Tyseley Church' as it was on the boundary. Built of yellow Rugby bricks with bands of red and blue bricks it was designed by Yeoville Thomason. The church dated back to 1820, when a Sunday School met in a granary near Yardley parish church, and was extended on its Stockfield Road site in 1895 to include gas fittings in the new school and enlarged church. In that year its thriving Sunday school provided the annual 'treat' of a picnic with swings, games, races and toys for every child who failed to win a prize, according to the *Yardley Newsletter*.

Acocks Green Old Choral Society met regularly in the Congregational church and one of the church's most well-known members was the Worcestershire Justice of the Peace, Mr Henry Piddell. The *Yardley Newsletter* relates that he "was a man of sunny temperament and ingenuous nature, associating himself with many of the social movements of the area". He attributed his success in life to his happy marriage, saying, "I always consult my wife in any matters of importance and consider she has been worth £500 a year to me all our married life"!

In 1863 another church was founded in Acocks Green, being the new Wesleyan Chapel on the Shirley Road which became the Methodist church. It was built on land owned by Thomas Bott who also constructed Bottville Road, later called Botteville Road. The chapel was completed in October 1863 but soon became too small by 1881 when Acocks Green became a 'middle-class Edgbaston'. A new chapel opened in 1883 which was lit by gas.

A fire in 1893 destroyed half of a schoolroom attached to the Wesleyan chapel. There was no local fire service at that time but luckily the Birmingham

Fire Brigade miraculously arrived with a steam engine within half an hour of receiving a telegram for help! In the Twenties the church deteriorated and after much fund raising the alterations took place in 1927. New schools were planned and funded for 1933 with many more financial appeals, one of which was a brick fund. Many locals purchased a brick on which their names were inscribed for posterity and a certain fee.

Acocks Green's Gothic-styled parish church was not built on the Warwick Road until 1866, with the church house being on Arden Road for many years. It was bombed in December 1940, with the roof being badly damaged and one pillar pitted with fragments. The vicar escaped injury as he was holding confirmation classes in a nearby shelter. The church was eventually rebuilt and celebrated its centenary in 1966.

Education in Acocks Green was provided in 1874 by St Mary's Church School in Broad Road. Mr Fieldhouse was the first headmaster, appointed on a salary of £75 per year and the scholars were charged 2d. per week. In 1879 new classrooms were built when attendance figures rose to 100 boys, 63 girls and 62 infants. By 1906 the Board of Education demanded urgent improvements to the school or immediate closure so appeals were made to raise money for the improvements.

In order to educate the growing population a new council school opened in 1908 on a site between Westley Road and Warwick Road. It once had been the site of Camden Lodge, the home of the Johnson family. An elderly resident recalls that in 1911 the Infant School headmistress was Miss Knott, and Mrs Tanner in the Junior School. All teachers were qualified graduates and there was a high educational standard. Pupils were never allowed in or out of school without their gloves! She also recalls that to the left of the school was an old fashioned row of cottages and a well-known sweet shop. Many pupils left their 'love letters' at the shop where the owner was known as 'Old Ma Bolton' — she provided a valuable service in those days when Acocks Green really was a village!

In 1878 Acocks Green's Institute was built on Sherbourne Road at the 'Five Ways' junction of Station Road, Oxford Road and Dudley Park Road. It was a magistrates court and meeting place for Yardley District Council as well as being a place for dances and public meetings and entertainments. Its ambitious aims were "the extension of literary, scientific and artistic knowledge, improvement in public speaking and debating and the provision of wholesale recreation for its members". No doubt it became an important part of social life in the area until it was demolished in 1965.

Other social organisations in the district, according to the 1895 *Yardley Newsletter*, included a thriving Poultry and Pigeon Society, the Liberal Club, Choral Society, Bowling Club, Working Mens Club, Cycling Club, Football Club, Rambling Club and Conservative Club. Tennis courts were available in Arden Road and Lyndon Cricket Club, founded in Clay Lane, thrived in Gospel Lane.

In the month of March in 1895 the district was buffeted by bad gales and a

'Five Ways', looking up Sherbourne Road – the junction of Dudley Park Road, Station Road and Oxford Road. The Institute is on the left of the photograph which was taken by George Lewis, c.1910. (M. Wood)

Sherbourne Road resident, Mr Hunn of Silverdale, suffered two large chimney stacks crashing through the roof. At the same time a large oak tree fell across the Yardley Road near the station and many roofs, fowl pens and chimney stacks were blown away. At Acocks Green Farm, "Mr Woodcock's monstrous elm, the largest for miles around, was uprooted, falling on two carts", states *Yardley Newsletter*.

In 1897 Queen Victoria's Jubilee was celebrated by a fete with maypole dancing. Children gathered on Station Fields, beside the station, and received a flag or a fan. A procession in fancy dress paraded to Knights Field, on the site of Mayfield Road, where each child was presented with a souvenir book of the Queen's reign and was treated to an afternoon of sports and games.

At the turn of the century the Warwick Road near the Olton boundary was very rural and was virtually the end of everywhere. The Spread Eagle was a well-known establishment near the Dolphin Inn, on the corner of what is now Victoria Road. It was the terminus of the old horse bus which left for Birmingham once an hour. Matt Bissell was the jovial landlord of this hostelry which was reputed for its good company and a sure welcome. Fine ale was 3d. a pint, the sawdust was fresh on the floor and good roast beef was available at the bar counter. The Spread Eagle was demolished in 1929 when the road was widened.

Victoria Road was built up with housing in 1928, with cornfields from the

Maypole dancing in 1897.

The Spread Eagle on the Warwick Road, c.1912. In the distance can be seen the Dolphin Inn. (M. Wood).

Dolphin Farm behind the back gardens. The Dolphin family were well-known in the area as was Mrs Severne, another local landowner commemorated by Severne Road. Dolphin Lane was little more than a cart track at the beginning of the century, as was Beeches Lane nearby, (originally called Walls Lane after the farmer whose building was on the corner of the Warwick Road by a duck pond). The whole of this area was in the heart of the countryside, with green fields full of buttercups, grazing cattle and sheep. Beeches Lane was later called Gospel Lane.

George Lewis took this postcard view of rural Acocks Green, c.1906. The sender of the card wrote that the view was of a "a favourite walk" – perhaps it was along Dolphin Lane.

AN EARLY MOTOR CHARABANC

In Gospel Lane Mr Griffin had his taxi service in the 1940's. His grandfather (from Sparkhill) had provided char-a-bancs for Stratford Mop.

Gospel Lane probably took its name from the Gospel Oak — a tree so large it took a team of sixteen horses to draw it away when it was cut down in 1846 by Colonel Smart. The oak marked the boundaries of Yardley, Solihull and Bickenhill and is commemorated by the Gospel Oak Inn. On Rogation Days the Beating of the Bounds took place at the Gospel Oak, when a portion of scripture was read and a psalm was sung underneath the tree. The boundary stones were beaten with boughs when the boundaries were crossed as part of the ceremony.

Gospel Oak Farm was tenanted by the King family for three or four generations. In the nineteenth century George King was in residence for seventy five years, well-known for his trade in horses to owners of carriers' carts and hop wagons which used to bring hops by road from Worcestershire and Kent. He also owned nearby Broom Hall House and farm. George King was buried in Hall Green church and his son Edmund King took over the tenancy of the farm until his death in 1897. During his lifetime the farm was the scene of "frequent conviviality and much hospitality", according to the 1911 *Acocks Green, Olton and Solihull Journal*.

In Gospel Lane in the 1940's Mr H. Griffin had his 'modern car service'. He was the grandson of W. G. Griffin, a cab proprietor from Sparkhill, who had originally been the only police officer in the parish of Yardley. An enterprising man, he had been one of the first firms to send char-a-bancs to Stratford Mop.

Further up the Warwick road towards Olton was Acocks Green Laundry. Its green vans were very familiar in the district with regular collections and deliveries, the neat brown paper parcels revealing clean laundered sheets and shirts, all beautifully pressed, and collars stiffly starched. Many people had their linen washed by this service in the days before washing machines became part of ordinary households. Nearby was Woodcock Lane, on the Rover Works site, where the Vineries grew large quantities of grapes in their market garden.

On the Shirley Road leading out of the village was an old farm and some cottages on the site of the present library. At Ivy Cottage Miss Elizabeth Osborn and her horse Prince once resided. The Shirley Road was very narrow and winding, bordered by hedges, and was not developed until the Thirties. Most roads in the district were of poor quality, the dust turning to mud in the rain so that early cars made life miserable for everyone at the roadside. An elderly resident of the Twenties and Thirties recalls that along the Shirley Road lived many distinguished people at one time — Alderman Sam Grey and his wife Jessie, Lord Bennett Lucas of Bennett Magneto factory in Acocks Green, Sir Kenneth Corley and Mr Beale-Brown of the Bank of England.

By 1911 Yardley Rural District was unable to cope with the demands for services in the rapidly expanding population of Acocks Green. The village at the turn of the century had lacked most of the necessities of urban life, including good road surfaces, drains, lights, baths, libraries, refuse collections and a good transport system. In 1911 the area joined Greater Birmingham which led to an increase in amenities, housing developments and road

Vineries Lane (now in Woodcock Lane) where there was a large market garden and vinery at the beginning of the century. The bridge crossed the Birmingham & Warwick canal which opened in 1799. (J. Marks).

improvements in the Twenties. Many council houses were erected which radically altered the social structure of Acocks Green. On the domestic front, piped water had reached Acocks Green by 1890 and mains drainage by 1900. By 1911 gas lighting was on the streets and in new houses.

The Outer Circle bus route included Acocks Green village in 1926 and the electric trams which had reached Flint Green Road in 1916 were extended down the narrow Warwick Road to the village in 1922. There had been some opposition by the locals to the invasion of trams on their quiet village, as they complained they were having to contend with "irresponsible cyclists and motorists and the prospect of tram cars will about complete the death trap which exists by the Council Schools", according to an article in *Acocks Green, Olton and Solihull Journal* in 1911. However, trams arrived and continued until 1937 when motor buses took over the service.

The increase in traffic in the Twenties caused quite a few accidents, although the earlier horse era had not been without its share of horrific disasters with many runaway horses and smashed carriages being reported in the press. A driver of a motor-car on the Warwick Road in Acocks Green was fined forty shillings in 1921 for dangerous driving at 20 miles per hour past a tram. This speed seems laughable to us nowadays but indicates how the motor-car so dramatically changed the pace of life for everyone.

Dorothea Abbott recalls an incident in the Twenties and relates her memories of that era:-

1913 advertisement in 'Acocks Green, Otton and Solihull Journal'.

These late seventeenth century cottages in Arden Road are Acocks Green's oldest surviving residences. (Acocks Green Library)

This postcard view of Arden Road in 1906 clearly shows the oak tree which was reputed to be one of the last from the Forest of Arden.

Near Flint Green Road, on the Warwick Road on the same side as the church, was a row of small brick cottages with tiny front gardens. In about 1928 there lived in one of the cottages a very old lady. She could often be seen, dressed in a crinoline and black bonnet, sitting on a chair outside her front door, watching the traffic go by. Next door to her lived Nurse Smith, the local district nurse who often cycled around the area. She used to wear the navy blue mackintosh uniform with a flowing head-dress. I remember the uniform was changed after another nurse was killed by her head-dress getting caught in the wind on her bicycle, resulting in her falling in the path of an on-coming car.

Nearby in Arden Road, are some very old seventeenth century cottages, probably the oldest in Acocks Green. An old oak tree on Arden Road was supposed to be one of the last oaks in the Forest of Arden, and was preserved on a specially built island in the road. Mr H. M. Cashmore, the City Librarian for many years, lived on the corner of Arden Road and Sherbourne Road. During World War II a land-mine dropped in his garden and he was so proud of it that he refused to allow the Public Works Department workmen to fill in the hole! He was a regular visitor to Acocks Green library, often taking friends and colleagues there as it became a show piece when it first opened in the Thirties.

What really made the day for us children in the Twenties was the thunderous advance of a steam roller, preceded by a man walking along

A postcard depicting the illuminated tram which was frequently seen in the Twenties. (J. Marks)

with a red flag. It made a glorious din, every part of it rattling and shaking!. We would crane our necks from our bedroom windows until it disappeared out of sight.

The Number 44 trams used to pass our house on the Warwick Road, near Fox Hollies Road, plying between Acocks Green and Dale End in the city. They made comforting patterns of light on the bedroom walls at night. On national occasions the Illuminated Tram came along when it was dark. Crowds would line the road waiting for this astonishing spectacle which was truly beautiful to our eyes.

We were in the unique position of living within fifteen minutes walk of three railway stations — Acocks Green, Spring Road Platform and Tyseley Junction. Acocks Green station, with its large commuting population, was said to be one of the busiest stations in the whole of the Great Western system. At busy periods it was not uncommon to see two snorting giants at the station at once, one going to Moor Street and the other to Snow Hill.

A travelling bagpipe player once came to play outside our house. My mother found all the small change she could for me to give him but I was so terrified of the strange man making the hideous noise that I just flung the pennies at him before rushing back into the house!

I first learned to lisp my ABC at Cofton House on Westfield Road, a private educational establishment which was run by Mrs Allen and her daughter, the beautiful red-haired Kathleen. We had a very strong grounding in our Scriptural Knowledge — I remember that the Sixty Four Dollar Question was "Who is it makes you do wrong?" Another child gave the correct answer, which was the Devil, which was just as well as in desperation I was ready with the name of the current Naughtiest Girl in the School! Apart from learning about the Devil we also learned a lot of poetry, Greek mythology and history. We learned our numbers by moving coloured beads along wires before graduating to arithmetic books with squared paper. We learned our tables together parrot fashion, but surprisingly it was fun. Gym was taken at St Mary's Church Hall in Rookwood Road.

School counting frame.

Other private schools of the period between the wars included the Convent School of Our Lady of Compassion and Wellesbourne House School for Boys, on the Warwick Road near the Red Lion. Opposite was Eastbourne House School for Girls, run by Miss Marshall, which later moved to the Yardley Road. There were also two private schools on Station Road, near the junction with Oxford Road and Dudley Park Road, called Cumberland College and The Hurst. Margaret Barnes, a friend of mine, recalls using slates and slate pencils at Cumberland House and a dreadful book of scripture extracts dealing mainly about death!

The teachers were mainly uncertificated at that time.

I moved on to Acocks Green Infants School on Westley Road which was jointly the local Institute at the time. This was not ideal as only a curtain divided two classes which must have been difficult for the teachers! Playground discipline was strict, especially for the boys who had to go 'to the wall' if they offended and to stay there for the duration of playtime. In the playground the girls chanted a rhyme about the school colours which were red and green — "red and green, kidney beans". This got into one of the Opie's books on childrens' games.

I graduated to the Elementary School on the Warwick Road, opposite Dudley Park Road, which was a red brick building. In a class of over fifty five children we were well taught by Miss Benington. The Headmistress was a portly lady called Miss Hill.

1911 advertisement.

Hazelwood Road, once Dog Lane, is a very pleasant road lined with trees and individual houses. An elderly resident recalls that one of the houses, now replaced by a block of flats, was once owned by the German Consul during the First World War and that some bitter person painted red crosses on the iron gates. She also recalls that there was a house and paddocks owned by the Moody family, which was built over in 1925/6 with municipal flats and houses (Numbers 76 – 104). There were cows in the field at the back. During the Depression houses were available there with government subsidies so that one could be purchased with £600 and a £100 subsidy. Hazelwood Tennis Courts were once on the site of Hazeltree Croft and the Wesleyan Tennis Courts and Bowling Greens were on the site of Green Acres.

There was once a business in Hazelwood Road called Hazelwood Nurseries which sold plants and fresh tomatoes until the Sixties, when flats were built on the site. Connie Hawkes remembers that during World War II the road was often the target of German bombers who probably mistook the reflections of the windows of the Nurseries for the Rover factory in Solihull. This often happened during the period of full moon — "the bombers' moon" — when pilots thought the reflections came from the canal which flowed past the Rover works. She also recalls seeing Greenwood Avenue lit up one night when chandelier flares were dropped which was a wonderful sight in spite of the danger.

Another resident recalls vividly the bombing of Hazelwood Road in August

1940. A bomb landed on the Wesleyan Tennis Courts and all residents of nearby houses had to be evacuated for two or three weeks. The bomb was eventually removed after six weeks by Bomb Disposal Squads, with great difficulty as the six foot long device kept sinking into moving sand. She also recalls that in November 1940 a land mine completely wrecked Number 83, causing several deaths and casualties. Five houses were damaged and nearly all were roofless and windowless. The A.R.P. help was magnificent.

Acocks Green has seen many changes since the Forties and is now a thriving suburb in the city of Birmingham. In 1903 the *Birmingham Daily Mail* spoke of Acocks Green's "wealthy residents who had loved the place for its quiet exclusiveness and pleasant detachment." Perhaps it is not the place it was a century ago but it is still a pleasant locality and is within easy reach of both the city and the countryside in these days of fast modern transport.

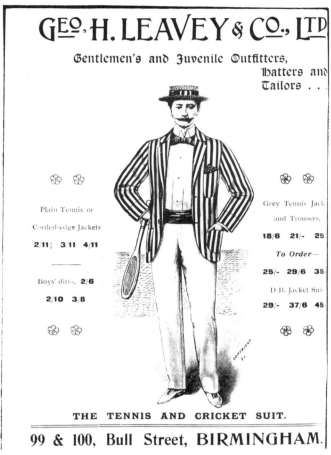

Advertisement in Acocks Green and Solihull Journal, 1900

CHAPTER 14

ACOCKS GREEN VILLAGE CENTRE

The village centre of Acocks Green, known first as Westley Brook, developed around 'The Green', a triangular piece of land which eventually became the tram terminus before the current traffic island. Photographs at the turn of the century show the Warwick Road in the village with very little traffic, when life must have been much more pleasant for pedestrians.

For over twenty four years in the second half of the nineteenth century the village postman was Thomas Harris who seems to have become an entrepreneur as he also ran the newsagents, library and grocer's shop! He was one of the best known inhabitants of the area when he died in June 1895 at the age of sixty seven years. The post office was situated next door to the present one and had a blue brick forecourt which was up three steps behind a low wall.

The first police station in Acocks Green was on the Warwick Road at the bottom of the hill, on the site of the present school. It was a well-known establishment with its iron railings and moved in 1909 to a magnificent new building on the Yardley Road near the railway station. Adjacent to the old police station was the one-man fire brigade which was a local landmark with its hand propelled fire escape. Perhaps this was in addition to George Muscott's fire brigade at the tannery which was at the service of the district for a fee. A new fire station eventually opened later on in Alexander Road.

In the centre of the village were Westley Brook cottages, two rows of dwellings with gardens head-to-tail. They backed on to the old New Inn and were once badly flooded to a depth of six inches. The present New Inn is some distance from the old building. One of Mr Acock's old cottages may have been sited on the present traffic island where there was a row of cottages occupied at one time by a cab proprietor and a firm of tailors at the turn of the century.

The Midland Bank building is prominent along the Warwick Road and was built in 1903 for the Metropolitan Bank, featuring clearly on many old postcards. No doubt it was very necessary for all the shops trading in the village. By 1895 there were at least twenty five shops.

Mr J.V.Tustin gives us some idea of the shops around at the turn of the century, in articles entitled "Acocks Green fifty years ago" in the 1953 *District Advertiser*. Some of the ones recalled were Martin's the Pork Butchers, Harris Brothers the Shoemakers, Tustin's the Grocers and Clifford's the Butchers. Mr Clifford's large private residence adjoining his business became the West

The horse bus coming through Acocks Green village, 1906. On the left was Johnson the chemist advertising photographic appliances and chemicals. Across Station Road was George Lucas the baker, Henry Patterson the butcher and George Birch the newsagent who sold many postcard views of the village.

Midlands Gas Board and the Municipal Bank. Other shops at this time were Howell the Grocer, Hammond the Draper, Thornton the Fishmonger and Stubbs the Chemist, all names now long gone.

Harry Patterson the Butcher and Clifford's the Butchers regularly displayed at Christmastime much beef and mutton obtained from the Bingley Hall Cattle Show. Their premises were illuminated outside by huge incandescent gas lamps which highlighted a boar's head, complete with an apple in its mouth and decorated with holly and mistletoe.

In the house next door to the Red Lion was a tiny telephone exchange with its red enamel sign showing a bell with the words "Edison Bell Telephones". The Red Lion had a drinking trough outside for horses and a smaller one underneath for dogs. From the Red Lion the road at the turn of the century was narrow, with high trees and hedgerows. There were also three big houses with massive gates, one being occupied by Mr White who offered a £5 reward to local drunks to abstain from alcohol for a year, as he was a great supporter of teetotalism. Presumably the drunkards came from the Red Lion but history did not record if his offer was ever accepted!

Beyond the houses was Wellesbourne House School which flourished under headmaster Oswald Sunderland and assistant masters Herbert Dixon and Mr Whitechurch, who both became headmasters in the future. Another local

1900 advertisements.

1911 advertisements.

school was called Miss Marshall's School for Young Ladies.

Mr J. V. Tustin's father's shop was on the far side of Wellesbourne Drive and was a tiny shop in 1903 with well worn steps, until it was enlarged in 1938. Another shop mentioned in J. V. Tustin's articles was Lucas' Cake Shop on the corner of Station Road at the turn of the century. In the first house down Station Road was the well-known character Johnson the Sweep and his son Bill. Their float was drawn by a white pony which was usually soot black!

On the other corner of Station Road at that time was Bridges the Corn-merchants which was eventually demolished to make way for the old Picture Playhouse which opened in 1913. The cinema had seating for over five hundred patrons and was rated as one of the best suburban picture houses of the period. It had an ornamental exterior and was well-designed inside with hot water heating, artistic wallpaper, plush carpets and furnishings. Admission prices were from 2d. to 1/- in its short life in the silent films era. Picturegoers were even offered free cups of tea at afternoon performances! It never went over to sound and closed in 1929, showing for its last film "Man, Woman and Sin", starring John Gilbert.

The Warwick Road in Acocks Green village, 1911. On the right can be seen the Metropolitan Bank, Edward Pitt the florist, George Clifford the butcher and his house next door called 'Mossmere'. On the left is Lloyds Bank, Harris Bros the boot and shoemakers and Alfred Walker, the cycle manufacturer displaying the 'Garage' sign.

1912 advertisement.

Next door to the Picture Playhouse was Daw's the Fishmongers which is well remembered by local residents, including Dorothea Abbott who narrates her memories of many shops in the Twenties and Thirties:-

Daw's fish shop used to have pheasants and poultry hanging up in full feather, together with rabbits on hooks at the front. It did not have any windows and was open to the elements, smelling rather fishy with lots of sawdust on the floor. A great deal of chit-chat went on between all the members of the family who served at the counters — there was one counter for fish and one for eggs. Mr Daw used to keep all his money in a little cubby-hole at the back of the shop.

Near Woolworth's on the Shirley Road was another fish shop called Pearce's, which also sold game. Mr Pearce started his business by pushing a handcart from the Birmingham Fish Market to Acocks Green. From such small beginnings he had a really thriving business and in the Forties was advertising "Severn salmon a speciality". Tustin's shop also sold fish and was advertising in 1947 — "Fish fresh from the lochs — fillets of cod at 1/11, plaice 3/9".

By the Red Lion there were two drapers shops, one being called Manchester House which always seemed to have a bevy of pretty assistants. Opposite was a more superior 'up-market' establishment called Madame Florence's. Drapers and some other shops had an overhead cash system. If change was required the money was inserted with the receipt

Acocks Green Picture Playhouse on the Warwick Road near Station Road, designed by architects Hipkiss and Stephenson in 1912 and now demolished.
(Acocks Green Library)

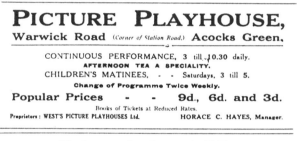

Playhouse advertisement, 1914.

into a cash container and sent on its way to a lofty being who sat in a little glass counting-house. This god would stash the bill to a spike and send the change in the container to the appropriate counter. As children we would happily watch this for hours!

In the Twenties and Thirties shopping was a much more leisurely affair than it is today. Grocers provided chairs at their counters so that housewives could sit down to give their weekly order, with a few helpful suggestions from the shopkeeper. As children we would stare entranced at the bacon-slicing machine and watch as the assistants poured sugar or rice from little shovels into thick blue paper bags. The bags were weighed on scales and the ends of the bags deftly sealed, without the aid if sellotape, of course! We would hardly have reached home before the grocer's boy would come panting up with the order carried in a box which was loaded on to the front of his bicycle.

My mother patronised Findon's Grocers shop which survived through
the Twenties and Thirties. There was also Wrensons' at the corner of
Dudley Park Road and Warwick Road, Clissold's on the Shirley Road
near Woolworth's and George's by the post office, so if one shop was
busy you could usually find one which was quieter.

Prices seemed to remain static which was a bonus, with a reel of cotton
costing 1d. for example. My mother always knew exactly how much she
would be spending on meat or fish. Woolworth's only sold articles
costing 3d. so it was an absolute mecca for children spending their pocket
money.

There were several butchers who always had sawdust on the floor —
Tustin's on the corner of Station Road, Wheeler's in the centre of the
village, Dipple's near the Shirley Road and Soden's near Station Road.
Mr Soden lived for many years next door to Margo Headford and
obligingly brought her a choice cut of meat every week, even when his
business moved to Knowle.

*Typical shopkeeper in the
Thirties.*

Delivery boy. (Punch, 1941).

As a child I remember the chemists having large bottles of brightly
coloured liquid at the top of their windows. They were very decorative
and gave the shop a mysterious air. Chemists which come to mind are
Needhams on the site of the old Picture Playhouse, Hedges by the
roundabout near Westley Road and Heaton's just past the Red Lion.

A tiny shoemaker's shop called Gilbert's always smelled of leather
which I remember well. As a child I always thought the old man who ran
it was very clever at finding your shoes when you collected them — he
seemed to know where every pair was on his shelves!

Acocks Green had several cake-shops in my childhood — one was
Wassell's, between Daw's fish shop and Lines' newsagent, which was run
by two fat ladies. A Miss Trillow ran another shop in the village which
was later replaced by Wimbush's. In our childhood we used to make up
rhymes about "Miss Trillow as fat as a pillow" which we thought
hilarious!

My mother used to walk frequently from our house on the Warwick

1920s advertisements.

Road to the "4 o'Clock" cake-shop on the Yardley Road to buy her cakes. She said they seemed to have more cakes than other shops and were much nicer. People used to go there from miles around as their cakes were sweeter than those in other shops during the war years, perhaps because they had a good sugar ration. Perhaps the food

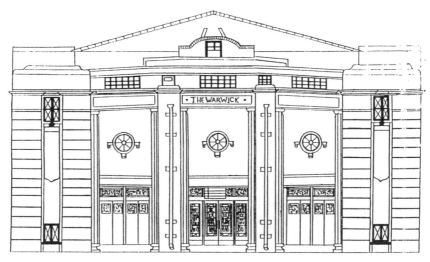

The Warwick cinema in Acocks Green, 1929 – 1991.
(Warwick Cinema (B'ham) Ltd)

ALDER BROS.

AUTOMOBILE   ENGINEERS

Repairs &
Overhauls
—
Cars
for Hire
—
Breakdown
Equipment
Etc.

Tecalemit
Official
Station
—
Power
Car Washing
Plant
—
Lock-up
Garages

WARWICK ROAD ∽ ACOCKS GREEN
BIRMINGHAM

Alder Bros. Garage in 1929 at 1200 Warwick Road. It later became W. N. Dixon's, Wyatt's Electrical shop and Busby's furniture store. (M. Clarke)

inspectors had taken pity on the two young girls who were making a valiant attempt in their wartime business venture!

In 1929 keen cinema-goers were able to patronise the new Warwick Cinema

Mr Wilfred Dixon's shop at 1200 Warwick Road was founded in 1933 in Alder Bros showrooms. Now trading as 'W. N. Dixon' and 'Logan Dixon' (fashion shops) it is pictured here in the 1940's, selling clothing, lino, carpets, mats at 1/ 11d., china and 26 piece dinner-services from 6/11d. It took two hours to set out this display and the shop was one of the first in the village to have a neon sign. (W. N. Dixon).

which opened on the Westley Road. It was designed to show the new sound films, replacing the obsolete Picture Playhouse. Music was provided by the Warwick Orchestra for many years for the audience of over a thousand. Prices of admission were 1/2 in the Circle and 6d. in the stalls. It closed for modernisation in 1962 and re-opened in 1964 as a cinema/bowling alley. Many locals will remember happy hours spent in the cinema in its heyday, before television altered the nation's viewing habits. Sadly, it bowed its head to the loss of audiences in December 1991 and closed down after showing its last film, aptly named, "Dead again". It has now re-opened as a 'laser experience' entertainment centre in line with modern trends.

In 1933 Wilfred Norman Dixon opened the first of his eighteen shops in the Midlands, at No. 1200 Warwick Road in Acocks Green (opposite the Dolphin Inn), being a business for ladies clothing and drapery. His business was based on a new budget account system, with customers originally paying 6d. a week, and has been so successful that he has been able to continue trading even during the current recession. A remarkable sprightly octogenarian, Mr Dixon still works full-time and ran the shops on his own until his son joined the business. Over the years he has traded at various neighbouring properties on

1930s advertisements.

the Warwick Road, including the well-known shoe shop and his store selling mens' and ladies fashions, trading under the name of 'Logan-Dixon' and 'W. N. Dixon'.

Mr Dixon recalls that in the Forties his shop sold mens' socks from 2d. a pair, pants and vests from 9d., 18-piece tea-sets from 1/11d. and rolls of lino from 9d. a square yard — measured, cut and delivered. No expense is spared to satisfy his customers, one of whom recently wrote: "It is so good to find a little corner of the world where one can receive such a courteous and delightful reception" — including free dahlia plants grown in Mr Dixon's garden!

This view of the tram and the bus terminus in Acocks Green, shows the library, New Inn and Warwick cinema between 1932 – 7. The poster advertises a special Sunday omnibus run to the Lickeys for 1/6. (J. Marks)

In the Thirties Birmingham Corporation began a new 'improvement scheme' in Acocks Green, planning a large central square at the junction of Warwick Road, Shirley Road and Westley Road with an island terminus for trams and buses. The old New Inn was demolished and a new one built. The Westley Road was widened with a number of old cottages being demolished between the Warwick Road and the Westley Road. The Shirley Road was widened with the derelict farmhouse and cottages in the village being demolished for the site of the new library.

The architect of the new library, Mr. F. J. Osborne, handed over a silver key to the Lord Mayor, Alderman J. B. Burman, at the grand opening ceremony on 14th June 1932. Large crowds gathered round the entrance to see the building which was reputed to be one of the largest branch libraries in the country as well as Birmingham's finest addition to its twenty five branches.

Special considerations had been made for plenty of light and it was solidly

1940s advertisements.

built with oak shelving for 23,000 leather bound books. In a Georgian design it had a spacious entrance hall, a magazine and newspaper room as well as a childrens' library. Wooden flooring was designed throughout the building which today would cost a fortune. Most important of all, it was designed on the new 'open access' principle, where readers could freely choose books from the shelves.

Within a couple of weeks the newspaper room was so popular with betting men that a complaint was made in a local newspaper about the noise they made discussing horses, even tearing away the strips of blue paper which had been pasted over the racing columns by library staff! This was in the days before betting shops were legalised so the library did its best to frustrate the activities of the bookies runners who tried to conduct their business in the newspaper room.

Dorothea Abbott remembers the excitement of her school classes who were marched along to join the library. They were issued with orange tickets and allowed to borrow only one book at first — fiction or non-fiction. Later on they were able to have two tickets but there was often trouble if anyone wanted to borrow two fiction books! She remembers going to the new childrens' library every day in the following school holidays.

Olive Price (nee Tonkinson) recorded her memories as a library assistant at Acocks Green library from 1937 – 1945:-

We considered ourselves lucky to work in this new show-piece of a library where the light airy atmosphere contrasted sharply with older city libraries. The library didn't close in the evenings until 9 p.m., except Wednesdays and Saturdays. We worked every minute of our thirty eight hour week with no tea- breaks!

Each morning our first job was to paste the strips over the newspaper racing columns. New pencils were issued only on production of the old one and recorded in the stock book. Books were issued for only two weeks and all renewals had to be entered in a book which caused a lot of work as did entering all fines in another book. We wore long green overalls which saved our clothes from dust and paste when clothing coupons were short. We made our own paste to stick on labels with packets of powder and boiling water, trying hard not to make it too lumpy!

During the war an appeal was made for books from the public and the staff room was filled with these books from all over the city. In the 1940 bombing raids we worked until the air raid siren sounded, usually at dusk, and then closed, getting home as best we could. All buses were stopped and wardens shepherded pedestrians into shelters.

When the boiler broke down one winter we just wore more clothing and carried on working in a temperature of 43 degrees, having only one electric fire behind the counter. There was a friendly co-operative spirit among the staff and I enjoyed working there.

1950s advertisements.

There must be many other people who have strong memories of wartime events and life in earlier years in the village. Acocks Green has continued to thrive and develop since the Forties but locals still refer to it as 'the village'or 'the Green' even though it is now a large suburb of the great city of Birmingham. Perhaps this account of the history of Acocks Green will stimulate others to delve into the vast resources of the Birmingham Reference Library to discover more of their heritage and to record for posterity their reminiscences of a bygone age.

CHAPTER 15

GLIMPSES OF OLD SPARKHILL

"In the nineteenth century there was a delightful place, where it was once a common sight to see small boys clutching jam jars full of minnows caught in the babbling brook which ran round the corner of Stoney Lane and the Stratford Road", related Mr V. Osborn in the 1921 *Sparkhill and District Weekly Advertiser*.

It is hard to believe that Sparkhill was ever such a peaceful country area in the County of Worcester — the brook mentioned formed a boundary between Warwickshire and Worcestershire. Within living memory the area changed from a sparsely populated rural district to one which rapidly developed into suburbia by the end of the nineteenth century. It became the population centre of Yardley Rural District which covered eleven and a half square miles, identical to the ancient manor and parish of the same name. The parish stretched from Sparkbrook to Olton, and from Shirley to Stechford, having its administrative centre in Sparkhill. It rapidly became part of the expansion of Birmingham, attracting businessman and workers from the city by the end of the nineteenth century.

Earlier history reveals that much of the land surrounding Sparkhill was owned by Maxstoke and Studley priories until the Dissolution of the Monasteries in the sixteenth century. Sparkhill may have derived its name from the Spark family of farmers who lived in the area in the thirteenth century. The Romans may even have been in the area earlier as two coins were discovered somewhere in Sparkhill.

The Greswolde family, Lords of Greet Manor, became landowners from 1562. Their manor house of Greet was built where the Greet Inn is situated on the Warwick Road. The Greswoldes also built Shaftmoor Farm, a three gabled half-timbered farmhouse, on Shaftmoor Lane. It was the home of the Steedman family for the last two centuries until it was demolished in 1929. The panelled rooms held secret cupboards and rich carvings. Packwood House, owned by the National trust, had some of its panelling. Adjacent to the farmhouse were Upper and Lower Fishponds, supplying the family with fish on Fast days. Members of the Greswolde family were baptised and buried in Yardley parish church.

Grove Farm was another old building which had been part of the Greswolde estate at one time. It stood on the Stratford Road near the River Cole, on the site of Grove, Greswolde and Nansen Roads in Sparkhill. The picturesque half-timbered structure was probably built in the early fourteenth century and extended in the seventeenth and eighteenth centuries. Originally called Fulford Hall, it was once the home of the Fulford family who took their name from the 'foul ford' in Formans Road.

Shaftmoor Farm.

Grove Farm which was demolished in 1898. (Birmingham Library Services)

The date 1654 was on one of the gables of Grove Farm. Another gable bore the initials of Henry Greswolde Lewis whose mother was the last of the Greswolde family. Henry Greswolde was the owner-occupier in 1840, also owning much of the surrounding land in Sparkhill at that time. On a third

Sampson Lloyd built 'Farm' in 1758 in Sparkbrook.

gable appeared the crest of the Fox family who were occupants at the end of the seventeenth century.

According to an article in the *Birmingham Weekly Post*, November 5th 1898, Grove Farm "had to bow its head to the requirements of a building society" in 1896 as the land was required for the site of "erections of a less comely appearance". During the rapid expansion of Birmingham at that time the farm was demolished in June 1898, despite the fact that it was an interesting architectural building. The last occupier was Mr J. W. Izod, the owner being Mr F. W. Greswolde-Lewis.

Other local farms included Woodlands Farm and Shrubbery Farm, the latter sited between Ivor and Esme Roads, becoming later Sparkhill Nursery. Sparkhill Farm on the Stratford Road was opposite Baker Street, surviving until the 1880's.

A large residence in neighbouring Sparkbrook was 'Farm', built by the wealthy Sampson Lloyd who founded Birmingham's first bank in 1765. His house is on the corner of Farm Road and Sampson Road and was considered to be one of the finest Georgian residences in Birmingham. He originally purchased 'Owen's Farm' in 1742, a Tudor farmhouse which survived until the Thirties. He then built 'Farm' in 1758, in front of which he planted a fine avenue of elms. The house now stands in Farm Park which is an oasis of calm in the busy streets of Sparkbrook, in an area which was once beautiful countryside.

The Angel Inn in the mid nineteenth century, with the toll-gates on the Stratford Road.

Stage coach.

Horsebus.

Sampson Lloyd's house 'Farm' had a beautiful pleasure garden. It included two summer arbours — one of which was called 'the fish house' by a pond and the other was in a more secluded situation, with windows of blue, green, yellow and purple glass. This delighted each successive generation of children — the blue windows when looked through gave a wintery appearance to the scene, green suggested spring, yellow the summer sun and purple the autumn. Inside the house were oak panelled rooms and a carved oak staircase. Among notable people who visited the Lloyds who were in residence until 1912 were Charles Lamb, Elizabeth Fry and Harriet Beecher Stowe, the author of 'Uncle Tom's Cabin' who visited ' Farm' in 1853.

Another notable house in Sparkbrook was Dr Joseph Priestley's home, called 'Fair Hill', which was on the opposite side of the Stratford Road to 'Farm'. It was originally owned by Sampson Lloyd and was surrounded by a fine meadow and a beautiful garden. Dr Priestley added a laboratory to the house and had a large library of valuable books. In 1780 he became minister of the Unitarians New Meeting Chapel, which caused him to become a major target for the mob of the so-called Priestley Riots in 1791 who demonstrated forcibly against the Dissenters. The mob drank all his wine and set fire to his house which burned down, with his laboratory where he had conducted experiments in electricity, oxygen and soda water. His work of twenty five years was destroyed, along with his books and his home. He sailed for America where he died in 1804 and is commemorated by a statue in Birmingham's Chamberlain Square.

A less elegant building but well-known in the district was the Angel Hotel on the Stratford Road in Sparkbrook. This was once kept by landlord Tom Parker whose dog, John Bright, was known all over the district. Near the hotel on the opposite side of Ladypool Lane (now Ladypool Road) stood a small white toll-house. The tollgates in the 1840's can be seen in an old painting of the Angel Hotel.

Most of the clay roads in the district were notorious in the eighteenth century for their bad surfaces and poor drainage until the Turnpike Trusts created toll-gates at the Mermaid, Greet Mill and Acocks Green.

A stage coach service from Birmingham to London had been provided by 1731, taking two and a half days to complete the journey — "if God permits", added the advertisement! By 1836 the roads had improved slightly, enabling horse-drawn coaches to travel from Birmingham to London in twelve hours, including stops. This was a great improvement on the earlier coaches which had only travelled at three miles an hour. It was always a hazardous journey with footpads haunting the turnpikes and highwaymen on the roads. In fact, many travellers considered it wise to make a will before travelling in a coach which "groaned, creaked and lumbered with each tug of the horses, as a ship rocking in a heavy sea over the contending waves", as a contemporary writer described it in Dent's *Old and New Birmingham*. The roads were often full of huge holes, deeply rutted with long patches of thick mud and rocky uneven surfaces which jolted the carriages unmercifully.

In the mid nineteenth century the Stratford Road in Sparkbrook was bordered by fields as far as Stoney Lane in Sparkhill. The only means of getting into Birmingham was by private transport, mail coach or horse omnibus. The omnibuses were owned by Mr Abraham Whitehouse, landlord of the Shakespeare Hotel on the corner of Henley Street.

The buses ran from the Mermaid Hotel, from the town side of the tollbar, commencing in the 1860's or 1870's. They ran to Moor Street, each coach accommodating only eight people on seats upholstered with crimson velvet, the floor being covered with straw. The cream coloured coaches must have been a fine sight as the guard blew a horn before leaving the Mermaid, continuing to blow almost all the way into town. Fares were 3d. outside, 4d. inside and the buses were drawn by three or four horses which were stabled at the Shakespeare public house. Abraham Whitehouse was a well-known character until his death in 1931. He developed the horse bus service along the Stratford Road and also ran a Sunday service as far as Solihull in 1875. Later horse buses were much larger with a top deck.

Turnpikes were abolished in 1872 so that horse buses from Birmingham to

The old Mermaid Inn in Sparkhill which was demolished at the end of the 19th century. (Yardley Newsletter)

Sparkhill became more frequent. The Mermaid Hotel became a local landmark standing at the junction of the Warwick and Stratford Roads. The building which we see today was a new one erected in 1895, but was originally a three storey building with a farmhouse at the side. It dated back to 1675 or earlier, when the property belonged to the Dolphin family in the reign of Charles II. The house and lands became known as 'The Mermaid' by the 1750's and was conveyed by deed to Joseph Smith, a Birmingham merchant, and Benjamin Taverner of Yardley, whose family held it until the end of the nineteenth century.

The adjacent fields belonging to the old Mermaid were named 'The Sparklings' and there was a triangular plot of land in front of the inn for many years. After 1834 the Mermaid became famous for its Tivoli Tea Gardens where cages of singing birds were kept in the beautifully kept grounds and it became popular with young people. The old Mermaid was always known as a house of good character and was renowned for its hospitality, especially at Christmas time. It stood rather isolated apart from a few scattered dwellings and a nearby farm. Coroners of the district held their inquests at the inn until 1894 and even confined prisoners there at times.

The adjacent turnpike gates near the Mermaid hung across the Stratford and Warwick Roads until 1872. The tollhouse dated back to 1856, with the right for collecting tolls being sold by auction each year at the Swan in Henley-in-Arden. The tollhouse keeper had an income from a weighing machine which

The New Mermaid Hotel, opened in 1896. (Yardley Newsletter)

was attached to the premises of the Mermaid. Carters paid a fee to have their produce or materials weighed and certified, which provided a considerable income towards clearing the rent for the Mermaid inn.

In 1896 Messrs. Showell Limited erected the new Mermaid Hotel, designed by the architects Wood and Kendrick, on the site of the old inn, realising the business potential of a modern new building on a prime site in the important part of the recently formed parish of Yardley. On the edge of rapidly expanding Birmingham it was a modern building, standing on an acre of land and providing an imposing sight with its two octagonal turrets, (which were bombed in the Blitz), terra-cotta cornices and massive gablings. In the centre gable was an ornamental panel showing a large figure of a mermaid which was a popular and favourite sign of the time.

Inside the hotel were walls lined with glazed tiles, mosaic tiled floors and richly coloured leaded-light windows. A symbol of the latest technology, it included electric bells and a telephone. There were three entrances to the large bar which was fitted out regardless of expense, with massive granite columns, elaborate arches and a mahogany bartop. Innovative features included the wholesale bottle department, a billiard room and a "ladies room comfortably furnished and fitted with lavatories exclusively for their use. This will, no doubt, be appreciated by the New Woman who is taking up a variety of amusements and employments hitherto monopolised by men", enthused the 1896 *Yardley Newsletter.*

Also included in the hotel was a kitchen fitted with gas stoves "capable of cooking sixty-eight pounds of meat at one time." No doubt the owners were aiming to attract much new business with the increase in commercial travel,

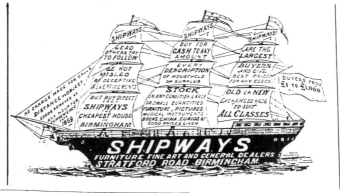

1898 advertisements.

providing an experienced chef, some sleeping accommodation for the public and ample stabling for visitors' horses. Nearly a century later the building is now under threat of demolition and stands empty, after having been a landmark in Sparkhill for so many years.

Up to the 1890's the area previously known as Spark Hill was very rural, dotted with cottages such as Holly Cottage in Court Road and Dell Cottages on Showell Green Lane. Sparkhill developed so rapidly that Rev. F.Hubert Ward, the vicar of St John's church, wrote: "The rapidity with which the ground at Sparkhill becomes covered with bricks and mortar is bewildering. Green fields are vanishing in every direction and new roads are to be cut all round the schools with a view to surrounding them with houses".

In 1897 two hundred and eighty houses were built in six months. The population explosion of the parish is self evident in the figures of the parish which rose from 17,000 in 1898 to 30,000 in 1907, although these figures included Greet, Springfield and Sparkhill. Most of the housing was for the large number of industrial workers flooding into the area as it developed. Much of the surrounding land was owned by the Smith-Ryland family, with road names commemorating them.

Education had been provided by Sunday schools in Bard Street by 1860, financed by Mr Thomas Lloyd of the Grange in Sparkhill. By 1890 the school had been taken over by the Yardley School Board which also provided College Road School in 1900, followed by Formans Road School and Golden Hillock School.

St John's School had begun even earlier in a villa in 1856 and was rebuilt in 1884 on a site on the Stratford Road donated by Yardley Charity Estates. Over £900 was raised to build the school, the foundation stone being laid by Lord Randolph Churchill, Member of Parliament. Fees at this voluntary school were 3d. a week. The Headmasters's wife, Mrs Baker, was well known as 'the Penny Woman' as she always paid shop-keepers in penny coins which had been collected at the school for her husband's salary. Mr Baker kept all his pennies in a water jug in his bedroom until the 1891 Education Act decreed that education should be free!

St John's church opened in Sturge Street (renamed St John's Road) in 1878, being known as the 'iron church' because of its galvanised iron roof. It was rebuilt after 1888, a generous benefactor being Miss Louise Ryland who donated £1000 to the fund just two days before her death. Another local church was St Christopher's in Springfield Road which was built later in 1906 in a new developing area near College Road Board School.

In 1895 the cultural needs of the parish were catered for by the provision of Sparkhill, Greet and South Suburban Institute, founded on the Stratford Road/ Newton Road corner. Councillor Malins was instrumental in persuading Worcestershire County Council to provide a £600 building grant. The Countess of Dudley laid the foundation stone in 1894 and the Institute opened in December 1895 in the presence of Austin Chamberlain, Member of Parliament. It included seven classrooms and a 75 foot lecture hall. Regular programmes were held for lectures, debates, concerts and all sorts of public entertainment.

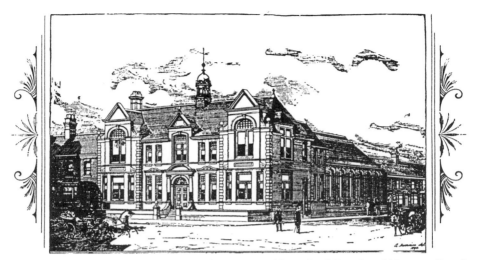

Sparkhill and Greet's Institute on the corner of Stratford Road and Newton Road, Sparkhill, 1895.

TUESDAY, JANUARY 5TH, 1897.

Children's Ball.

(Under the direction of Mr. H. AUSTIN.)

Tickets for Children under fifteen years of age, 1s. each.
Adults   ...   .   1s. 6d.   ,,

Adults are respectfully requested NOT to commence dancing until Ten o'clock.

1897 advertisement, Institute event.

Councillor Joseph Malins was a well-known man in the district at this time and did a lot for the parish of Yardley. "He is a power at County Hall and nothing seems to damp his indomitable ardour for every project undertaken — all bearing evidence of the touch of a master hand", stated the *Yardley Newsletter* in 1895. He was also on the board of the Yardley Charity Trust which donated land Yardley R.D.C. for use as public parks. Sparkhill Park, with its swings, roundabouts and pool was much loved by children in the area. It opened with great celebrations in 1902, which included a procession of Yardley Charity Trust governors, councillors, the Fire Brigade, a band and a squad of the Warwickshire Yeomanry.

Sparkhill Council House, on a very quiet Stratford Road, c.1911. In 1923 it became the Public Library. (J. Marks)

Council meetings were held in Sparkhill Institute after the Yardley Rural District Council had been formed in 1894, until the magnificent Council House was opened in 1902. This imposing building with a clock tower on the Stratford Road in Sparkhill is still a local landmark and was designed by Arthur Harrison, a Birmingham architect and built by William Bishop of Kings Heath. It included offices for the general clerk, the surveyor, the rate collector, the sanitary inspector and the medical officer of health. The wide stone staircase led to the large Council Chamber which was lined with wood panelling. At the rear of the building was the fire station, depot, mortuary and caretaker's house. Stabling for two horses was provided in the fire station which had two engines. In the depot there were stables for nine horses and a harness-room, a fodder store, cart sheds, a wheelwright's shop and a smithy. The total estimated cost of the building was £11,000, states *Building News, 30 March 1900.*

Yardley Rural District Council was responsible for roads in the district which were in an appalling state, as the 1895 *Yardley Newsletter*

1900 advertisements.

1900 advertisements.

reported: "It does not require any boundary mark on the Stratford Road for pedestrians to know where the city of Birmingham commences, for that part which is under management of Yardley authorities is about as bad as it can be. Both horse and footways are perfect quagmires of mud and water and those who are compelled to use them are sincerely to be pitied"!

Plans for paving roads got under way in 1896 but in comparison with services in Birmingham local residents got a bad deal as there was no refuse collection or drainage system and street surfacing was totally inadequate. Birmingham supplied water, gas and transport and in 1911 offered to provide

Stratford Road, Sparkhill, with the junction of Showell Green Lane on the left. The view shows a steam tram and a handcart owned by Thomas Lewis, the photographer, who used it to carry his plate camera apparatus, c.1905. (J. Marks)

all other services needed in Sparkhill. This tempted locals to vote in favour of joining Birmingham, especially as reduced rates were promised for fifteen years. The city authorities had the enormous task of providing all the services lacking in an area which reached as far as Hall Green and Acocks Green.

Most roads in the district had to be drastically improved for motor and tram transport. Some roads were narrow and winding and had a thick coating of dust which turned to mud in rain. Along the Warwick Road from the Mermaid humped bridges had to be strengthened and a weighbridge was used to ensure road engines were not too heavy. Early cars made life a misery for all pedestrians although the vast majority of people in Sparkhill used trams to travel into town to work. Steam trams which had reached Sparkhill by 1885 were soon replaced by open-topped electric trams which caused the demise of the horse buses. However, for some years at the beginning of this century horse-drawn vehicles existed beside the trams and early motor vehicles, causing chaos on the roads.

Few rural areas have changed as rapidly as Sparkhill, to become a prosperous residential district in such a short time. The development of Birmingham and its industries in this century has again caused another change in population in the last thirty years. There has been a tremendous increase in the immigrant population seeking employment and housing in Sparkhill, so that the area has changed yet again within living memory.

CHAPTER 16

ROUNDABOUT CAMP HILL

"There is not a prettier spot in the vicinity of Birmingham for a place of amusement or entertainment" ran an advertisement in 1785 in *Aris's Gazette*. There were clear views of the River Rea and the Lickey and Clent Hills from the gardens of the inn which might surprise many a modern Brummie passing through Camp Hill today. The advertisement related to the Anchor Inn, better known by its later name, the Ship Inn.

The Anchor Inn had been converted from an old farmhouse in about 1754. It was a two storey half-timbered building which had accommodated Prince Rupert in 1643 during his famous march through Birmingham. As proof of its existence in the sixteenth century an oak beam was found over the fireplace in the kitchen which was dated 1560.

In 1785 the inn stood in eight acres of grounds which included kitchen and pleasure gardens. As it was only ten minutes walk from town, it became a popular venue for afternoons or evenings. Another advertisement in 1796 gives the following account of the grounds: "The garden is laid out in great taste with arbours and seats and is exceedingly well stocked with fruit trees, shrubs and flowers, together with a kitchen garden of two and a half acres."

Changing hands in about 1786 the inn became known as the Ship Inn when a Mr Wood became landlord. He had been in the merchant navy and apparently wished to retain his title of Captain in a suitable environment. A few years later the inn suffered an attack by rioters during the Priestley Riots but survived.

The old Ship Inn was rebuilt in the nineteenth century with a blacksmith's forge adjoining it. In the window of the inn there was a model of a ship which was a great source of interest to all small boys as few had ever seen a ship in full sail at sea. Outside stood a long bench which was used by locals as a meeting place. Very few local people were able to buy a newspaper in the nineteenth century so it became a popular venue for men to meet on Sunday evenings at the Ship Inn to read the weekly newspaper which had been published in London the previous day and delivered there by stage coach.

The inn became a popular centre for many meetings and speeches from the horseblock in front of the building, in the days which preceded the Victorian Reform Bills and Corn Laws. John Bright and Joshua Scholfield, two Birmingham Members of Parliament, both made speeches there, after which

This illustration appears in T. Turner's History of the Ship Inn 1863, showing the forge and original date of the building.

Thomas Lewis, the Sparkbrook photographer, took this view of Camp Hill and the Ship Hotel at the turn of the century. A horse bus can be seen on the left hand side and a tram in the centre of the road. (J. Marks)

teas or suppers were served under the trees. It must have been a pleasant place surrounded by green fields and trees, apart from a few scattered houses and the Salutation Inn nearby.

The Ship Inn was rebuilt yet again to become the Ship Hotel which was a landmark in Camp Hill until it was demolished in the 1980's. It had a small statue of Prince Rupert above the door, with the words "Prince Rupert's Headquarters, 1643", which always intrigued Margo Headford as she wrote:-

Prince Rupert of Bohemia was not only a handsome and dashing prince but one of the most able soldiers of his age. For a long time he was the chief Royalist cavalry general for his uncle, Charles I, in the Civil War.

He believed implicitly in his favourite shock tactics for his Cavaliers and a terrifying sight he and his army must have been to the one hundred and fifty men entrenched at Camp Hill on that day in 1643. With Rupert galloping at the head of his flying horsemen, no doubt all waving swords and uttering fiendish yells, the poor citizens of Birmingham were no match at all for an army ten times their number. There were some casualties, however, on the Royalist side and it has been recorded that Rupert was incensed by the token defiance of the opposition, as he had been promised a safe passage through the town in order to help the King's forces in Lichfield.

Prince Rupert.

But Birmingham's sympathies had always been for the Parliamentarians and it had always been eager to make swords for them in its smithies at the crossing of the Rea in Deritend. Perhaps that is why Rupert turned a blind eye, after the successful battle, to the resultant wildness of his troops, who afterwards burnt houses with gay abandon, butchered some of Birmingham's leading citizens and terrified women and children. It has been said that much of it went on without his knowledge.

Although Prince Rupert can hardly be remembered with affection by Birmingham, he was a most loyal servant of the Crown, serving Charles I well in many battles. When Cromwell came into power, Rupert turned himself into a sailor and wreaked vengeance on the high seas. Charles II invited him back to court when the monarchy was restored and in his later years he once again became famous as a scientist as well as becoming proficient in the art of the mezzotint.

Although Camp Hill is generally thought to be named after Prince Rupert's encampment it may derive from Kemp Hill and the Kemp family who held land in the local Manor of Bordesley in the fifteenth century. However, Prince Rupert has long been associated with the area and his statue on the Ship Hotel stood forlorn and neglected for many months while the deserted building awaited demolition. Perhaps the statue has been preserved and cherished somewhere as an artefact of Birmingham's historical past.

CHAPTER 17

CHANGING SCENES OF LIFE

One of the chief pleasures of retirement must be that life no longer needs to be governed by time, as Margo Headford wrote:-

> If I were asked to give a congratulatory speech at a party for someone about to retire I would be inclined to make it go with a bang! I would present an old alarm clock to hurl on the floor or even out of the window!
>
> But for retired husbands there is sometimes too much time in the day! At first Maurice bounded into the garden and for a few weeks never stopped digging! Gradually it dawned on him that there was no need to hurry and I breathed a sigh of relief, having had visions of sciatica, lumbago or a slipped disc. It was pleasant to be able to go out at the drop of a saucepan when the sun shone. We enjoyed some walking in the countryside but I soon realised that Maurice needed something else in which to channel all his energy.
>
> Eventually he became involved in Hall Green Little Theatre, a nearby amateur theatre on Pemberley Road which had been built by hard labour and enterprise by a few enthusiastic members after World War II. There Maurice found a vocation, helping to make stage sets as he had always been quite a carpenter and had a flair for making something out of nothing. Not for nothing was he known in the family as 'Mr Fix It' as he was the proud possessor of a garage full of old junk, including screws and nuts dating back over forty years!
>
> At the theatre productions I soon found that my husband had accumulated an enormous circle of new friends — a great many of them ladies! I rapidly became a 'theatre widow' while he filled in the ocean of retirement time. He derived several years of great pleasure from his labours on the stage.

Margo and Maurice Headford much enjoyed rambling in the countryside in their retirement and she even bought her first pair of walking boots, as she relates:-

> I have become the proud owner of a pair of boots. Enormous, ungainly,

'Roses in the garden' at 52 Fox Hollies Road.

wet-proof, comfortable walking boots! I tried them out on some Warwickshire field paths in the wet and was delighted to find I could tramp through anything. I adopted a rolling gait not unlike a sailor, feeling I belonged to another generation. I was to bless my ungainly pieces of footwear on the next mountain holiday when my feet kept dry in a Welsh rainstorm on the rough terrain. Since then my boots have become treasured possessions over several holidays. I love them now with a fervent passion, though I doubt if I shall ever get my money's worth out of them!

A favourite excursion was Packwood House and the surrounding fields — "a perfect place in Warwickshire":-

It was whilst riding a bicycle in the early days of the Second World War that I came across Packwood House for the first time. I fell in love with it on sight although it was then owned by an industrialist and lay somewhat neglected and forlorn. But now it takes its ease, serene and cosseted by the National Trust.

The high walls of mellowed brick shelter visitors and the setting is so ideal that I should not be at all surprised if Henry VIII and all his court came striding on to the lawns! Most people come to see the enormous clipped yews, some thirty feet high, all of which are said to represent the Sermon on the Mount. In the grounds there are also many beehives and seven different kinds of sundials, as well as a lily pond and herbaceous borders to delight any gardener.

The back of the present house was originally the front and it is not difficult to imagine coaches travelling furiously down the fine avenue of trees, the horses arriving with steaming flanks at the substantial front door, with all the fuss and commotion that would ensue.

During the Civil War the owner, a certain John Featherstone, was so anxious about the fate of his house in those troublesome times that he is reputed to have sold horses both to the Royalists and the Parliamentarians, in an endeavour to keep it safe from harm. I know exactly how he must have felt. I would have done exactly the same!

Packwood House. (National Trust)

One pastime which gave her a lot of enjoyment was singing in Acocks Green Ladies Choir. She relates her memories of a typical concert:-

We chatter like starlings as we scramble onto the coach to visit the Darby and Joan Club. Underneath our coats we look more like penguins in our white blouses and black skirts.

Our conductor has wisely chosen a mixed programme to suit all tastes — a simple sketch, an amusing recitation, a duet perhaps as well as songs from the whole choir. We are fortunate in having one or two younger members although most of us are of pensionable age. One of the young ones, dressed in a bright shawl and a saucy hat on her auburn hair, sings "Wouldn't it be lovely" and the audience lap it up. Her little two year old girl, sitting nearby as good as gold with a bag of sweets clutched in her hand, claps enthusiastically at the end of the song. So do all those gnarled old hands.

Most of the ladies in the audience sit with half a smile on their lined and interesting old faces, quite ready to be pleased however bad we are! The few men cluster together in self defence in this predominantly women's world. They much prefer it when we roar out the "Viking Song" with it's "Clang! Clang! Clang! goes the anvil . . ."

Often there is a "muncher" in the audience with an inexhaustible supply of sweets in her pocket. Has she ever heard, I wonder, of Oscar Wilde's quip about the pleasures of old age? "They were", he said, "either illegal, immoral or make you fat!" I doubt if the first two concern her and she has long since come to terms with the latter.

Many of us are rapidly getting to that stage too as we gratefully accept the cups of sweet tea and cakes after the concert. Singing is thirsty work. We board our coach again after having satisfied and pleased our audience and one thing is certain — we have enjoyed it, anyway!

During her retirement years Margo Headford had many activities in Acocks Green, including pewterwork, embroidery, writing and passing an "O" level in local history at the age of sixty five which led to her becoming a founder member of Acocks Green Local History Society. Tennis continued to be a great source of pleasure at Dovedale Tennis Club in Lakey Lane in Hall Green and as a spectator at Wimbledon Lawn Tennis Championships. She also enjoyed voluntary work with local hospital trolley rounds and the "meals on wheels" services.

"Meals on wheels," by the author's 10 year old son. (N.E.S. Wilmot)

In 1981 disaster struck at the age of sixty eight. After a routine operation in hospital something went drastically wrong so that she lost the use of one leg, suffering numbness and pain for several months. Eventually things went from bad to worse and her pain increased, despite much medical treatment and assurance that her condition would improve. She gradually lost all mobility and independence in a world of relentless pain.

Life continued at home as best it could, with the assistance of the family, "meals-on-wheels", a zimmer-frame, home helps and a husband who increasingly became unable to cope due to his own declining health. Eventually life at home became impossible for them both and in 1989 they were admitted to residential care. Maurice died eighteen months later, sadly unaware that he had just passed his Golden Wedding anniversary. Reading has now become Margo Headford's only activity in her Nursing Home in the eightieth year of her eventful life.

POSTSCRIPT: As a Camp Hill 'Old Edwardian' Margo Headford attended a carol service in 1975 at her old school. She afterwards wrote an article in the school magazine which summed up her philosophy of life:-

At the service I couldn't help wondering what those confident and elegant sixth-formers really thought of us Old Girls sitting in front of them. It probably went through their minds: "We shall never get to that stage!". I hate to tell you — but it **will** happen, except that the old song is wrong! In "forty years on" most of today's pupils will be pretty spry! It's when you get to fifty or sixty years on that the body begins to creak and groan!

Can I impress on you the importance of going out and doing things before you settle down to make a home? Seize every opportunity that comes your way. Work hard for your chosen career but in leisure time go for the exciting and the unusual. I did and never regretted it! Those halcyon days with no real responsibilities will never come again!

We were not so fortunate as you in many ways. Education stopped at school if parents could not afford the higher variety. But we saw England and its beauties, as you will never see them, free from the enormous crowds that often ruin the things you go to see. We enjoyed the simple delights of hiking and biking in picturesque country lanes and although we hadn't much money, we had a great deal of fun in our unsophisticated fashion.

Biking 1930's.

Your opportunities are endless. Go to it and make the most of them!
Never forget you are only young once!

Margo Headford's life story became a school project a few years ago for for her grand-daughter, Debbie, and earned the praise of the teacher who commented that it would provide the raw material for at least one novel! It was, she said, "one of the most interesting family stories I have ever read. Your grand- mother has set you a high standard of industry, imagination and zest for living".

Maybe others will agree with the teacher's comment. If this account of life in a bygone age has entertained readers, as well as contributed to the local history of Sparkhill and Acocks Green, the book will have served its purpose.

Bibliography

ACOCKS GREEN DISTRICT ADVERTISER, 1946 – 53.
ACOCKS GREEN INSTITUTE PROGRAMMES,1897 – 1901.
ACOCKS GREEN, OLTON & SOLIHULL JOURNAL, 1900, 1911 – 14.
BICKLEY, W.D. Manuscript notes relating to the history of Yardley. 1926.
BIRMINGHAM ADVERTISER (SPARKHILL AREA). 1922/3.
BRYAN, M. P. A church's story: 130 years of Methodism in Acocks Green. 1991.
BULPITT, W. H. Historical account of Yardley Charity Trust. 1922.
CROFT, S. Stork wartime cookery book. 1940.
DENT, R. K. Old and new Birmingham. 1880.
HARDY, P. C & JACQUES, P. A Short review of Birmingham Corporation Tramways. 1971.
HOLDEN, B. Birmingham's working horses. 1989.
HUDSON, C. J. St Mary's parish church and the history of Acocks Green. 1966.
JENKINS, A. T. Story of the parish of Sparkhill. 1937.
JENSON, A. G. Birmingham transport. 1978.
LONG, P. 100 years of Sparkhill (St John's school). 1985.
LOWE, R. J. Farm and its inhabitants. 1883.
MINNS, R. Bombers and mash — the Domestic Front. 1980.
MORRIS-JONES, J. Acocks Green and all around. 1973.
"   Cole valley south. 1989.
"   Hall Green and hearabout. 1979.
"   Sparkhill and Greet. 1970.
"   Urbanisation of Yardley. 1968.
PONTIFEX, G. M. Short history of Acocks Green with some reminiscences of half a century ago. 1942.
PRICE, V. Birmingham cinemas. 1986.
RABOUGHAM, D. History of Acocks Green. c1970.
SMIRKE, R. S. Electro-plate trade. 1913.
SPARKHILL & DISTRICT WEEKLY ADVERTISER, 1921.
SPARKHILL,GREET & SOUTH SUBURBAN INSTITUTE PROGRAMMES, 1895 – 1912
SUBURBAN ADVERTISER & NEWSLETTER, 1924/5.
TURNER, T. History of the old Ship Inn. 1863.
TWIXT ROAD & RAIL: SCHOOL CHRONICLE (K.E.G.S. Camp Hill), 1923 – 8.
VICTORIA COUNTY HISTORY, Vol 3, Worcestershire.
YARDLEY NEWSLETTER, 1895/6.